CONTENTS

HEDGEHOGS

by Pat Morris

ÉAMON DE BUITLÉAR
WILDLIFE
BOOK 2

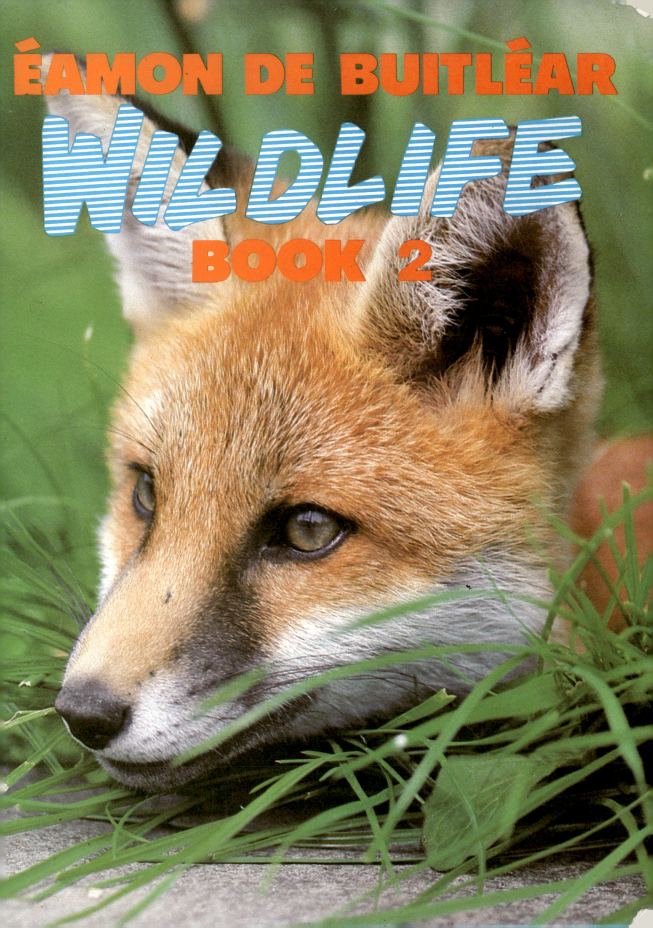

PREFACE

It scarcely seems a year since *Wildlife Book 1* was launched, and was so enthusiastically received by readers of different age groups. Once again, we in the Kerry Group are pleased to be associated with *Wildlife Book 2,* and it is clear that the series will continue for years to come. In the manner typical of a professional, Éamon de Buitléar has on this occasion surpassed even his exceptionally high standards to provide another information-packed and beautifully illustrated publication. Without doubt, *Wildlife Book 2* will provide hours of educational and informative entertainment to an ever-increasing number of young wildlife enthusiasts. Much credit and respect must go to wildlife bodies and organisations who do so much to preserve and protect our wildlife heritage in all its aspects. We in Kerry, by being associated with *Wildlife Books 1* and *2,* demonstrate further our concern for the preservation of this heritage, which we take into consideration at all stages of our commercial development.

Denis Brosnan
Managing Director
Kerry Group

ACKNOWLEDGEMENTS

Éamonn de Buitléar and the publishers are very grateful to the individual contributors to this book and to the following people and organisations for their help during its preparation:

Mr Rob Hume of the Royal Society for the Protection of Birds who provided all the colour sections of this book from previously published issues of *Bird Life* magazine, Mr Richard Nairn of the Irish Wildbird Conservancy for providing valuable advice on the choice of material and checking it for accuracy, Mr Richard Mills and Mr Cian de Buitléar for providing photographs, Mr Michael Drummey of the Kerry Group and Siobhán Parkinson who read the text.

Published by Country House, 2 Cambridge Villas, Rathmines, Dublin 6, Ireland

© Country House 1986

British Library Catloguing in Publication Data

De Buitléar, Éamon
  Wildlife book II.
  1. Natural history - Ireland - Juvenile
  Literature
  I. Title
  574.9415   QH143

ISBN 0-946172-07-2

Designed by Wendy Dunbar. Typeset by Glynis Millar. Printed by Criterion Press, Dublin.

Throughout Ireland the hedgehog is viewed with affection and amusement. It is one of our most familiar mammals.

The commonest way to see a hedgehog is dead on the side of the road. They are active at night and when dazzled by the lights of a car they roll up in a defensive position instead of running away. Many get killed this way.

Hedgehogs are found in most parts of the country where there is some ground cover.

Nor will the hedgehog harm pets. Fleas on cats and dogs are often blamed on hedgehogs, but the hedgehog flea is a special one which prefers not to live on other creatures. Cats and dogs have fleas of their own!

The hedgehog is our only spiny mammal. It has about 5,000 spines which defend it so well that a rolled-up hedgehog has little to fear from predators.

The spines are special, sharp hairs. They are not moulted at a particular season like normal fur. Each one grows and drops out after a year or 18 months.

Baby hedgehogs leave the nest at four or five weeks old. They are looked after only by their mother. Once the family breaks up they live alone. Four or five babies may be born, but many very young hedgehogs die. A female will often desert or eat her young if she is disturbed soon after giving birth. The mother finds it difficult to look after large litters and up to a fifth of the babies born may die before leaving the nest.

Hedgehogs usually come out after dark. This is because most of their food – worms, beetles and slugs – is easier to find then. They forage in woods, pastures and gardens but are uncommon on moors and in conifer forests. They return to a nest just before dawn – sometimes a different one each day. Apart from food, they need dry leaves to build a weatherproof winter nest in which they hibernate. They spend the whole winter asleep! A good place for a nest is under dense brambles, in thick undergrowth or under a shed. Town gardens should not be kept too tidy! If all undergrowth is cleared away and old leaves are burnt, hedgehogs are left with nowhere to spend the winter. Heaps of garden refuse are tempting places for hedgehogs. Be careful to check them for lodgers before lighting a bonfire!

Continued on P.80

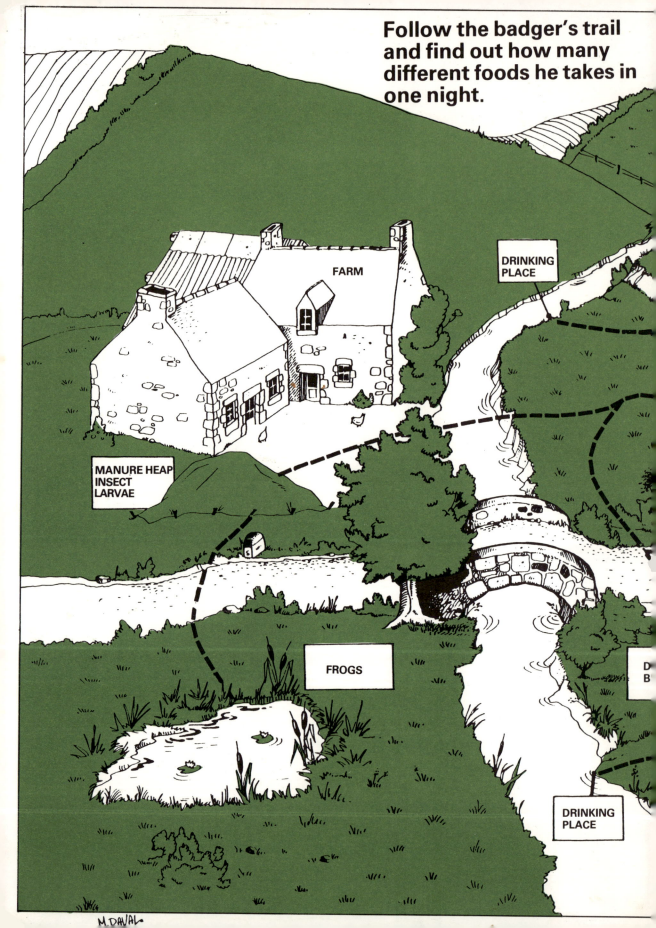

Follow the badger's trail and find out how many different foods he takes in one night.

DRINKING PLACE

FARM

MANURE HEAP INSECT LARVAE

FROGS

D B

DRINKING PLACE

M.DAVAL.

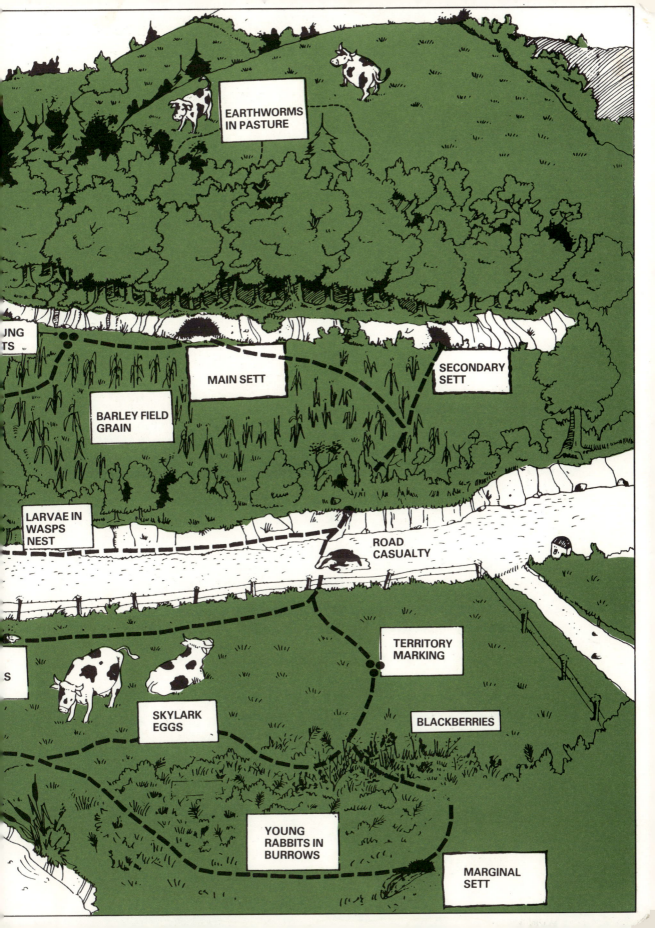

FISH

by Gwyn Williams

Fish are very specialised animals. They live in all kinds of water – fresh and salt, flowing and still. There are 20,000 fish species in the world. About 5000 live in fresh water. To any predator fish are a rich, energy-packed source of food. But the predator has to catch the fish and this is not always simple.

Fish have good eyesight, even in poor light. Many species have good hearing and of course they can swim. Most fish have a normal swimming speed and a faster 'sprinting' speed. This is used to escape danger or to catch food. A good sprinter, like the salmon, can cover a distance ten times the length of its body in a second but it soon gets tired. Many fish are well camouflaged. Some are even able to change colour to match their surroundings.

To overcome these difficulties, birds have had to develop special methods of catching fish. The basic problem is always the same – the bird has to be able to plunge into the water, find the fish and catch it, before it is able to get away.

Birds do not reduce natural fish stocks. If they did, they would soon have nothing left to eat. Usually the number of birds depends on how many fish there are, not the other way round.

Brown trout
The brown trout lives in many freshwater lakes and rivers. It likes to feed on the mayfly which flies about the water surface. The mayfly cannot survive in polluted water so when it goes the trout will suffer.

Pike
The pike is one fish that gets its own back and eats birds! The pike lies in wait for its prey, hiding amongst water-lilies or reeds. Then, with a powerful stroke of its tail, it dashes out to capture its food. It is usually another fish but, in summer, may be a young duckling, moorhen or coot.

Sand-eel and sprat
These are the main species of fish which our seabirds prefer for their food. Terns hover above the sea, then plunge down to catch them just below the surface of the

Continued on P.33

Left
Three-spined stickle-backs are very common. Males turn red beneath in the breeding season and build nests for the female's eggs.

Right
The pike is usually up to 50cm long and 1kg in weight. Some grow very much bigger.

Right
Brown trout may reach 100cm in length and a weight of 15kg.

Right
Mackerels are sea fish of up to 50cm in length. Along with herrings, they are the favourite food of gannets.

Right
Flounders can change colour to match their surroundings. In estuaries, flounders of 7-20cm form the main part of the diet of cormorants.

The step-by-step way of drawing frogs. Start with a large D drawn on its side, then add two circles for eyes. Keep on adding the parts shown under each frog. Now try the funny frogs below. Happy drawing!

D   OO

FROGS AND FROGS

CROAKING

CROAK

LAUGHING

HUMMING

MMM

LOOKING UP

SITTING ON A LOG

(BACK VIEW)

SITTING ON A LILY PAD   HIDING   WINKING

SINGING   SLEEPING   SMALL

S   WOG   GRUMPY   UPSIDE DOWN   TOP VIEW

FOCUS ON MOORHENS

by Irene Allen

Wherever there is fresh water, you will probably see a moorhen – but these shy birds are equally at home on land.

Worldspread

Moorhens are common over most of Ireland except in very high areas where the only water is fast-flowing, or there is no cover for them to skulk in. They like any still or slow-moving water, from small ditches to lakes, and are found in every continent of the world except Australia. Moorhens belong to the same family as coots, water rails and corncrakes.

Spring fever

In the breeding season pairs of moorhens defend a territory for feeding and nesting and are quite aggressive. They may chase off their own young once they are fully grown, but sometimes young of the first brood may look after the young of later broods. In autumn and winter adults are much less aggressive and chicks born late in the season may be allowed to stay with their parents until the next spring. When two pairs of moorhens fight, the two males and the two females usually fight each other.

Nests for all occasions

In early spring before building a cup-shaped nest for egg-laying, moorhens often build a platform of piled-up vegetation on which they can display to each other. Once the eggs in the true nest have hatched, the parents may build another 'brood' nest for the young to use. For a second brood, they either build yet another nest, or improve the first one.

High rise nests

Moorhens usually nest quite low down, among the bankside vegetation or on a low branch hanging over the water. But nests have been found up to eight metres high in bushes and trees – sometimes in old nests of magpies or woodpigeons. Floating nests are built on a platform of twigs and those in water deeper than 20 cm usually have a ramp leading up to them, making it easier for the birds to climb up.

Hold tight

When danger approaches, moorhens often dive underwater and grasp a piece of weed with their feet to hold themselves under. The only part that shows above water is the tip of the bill which acts as a snorkel.

Merely moorhens

It seems strange that a bird that spends all its time on or near water should be called a moorhen. The old name of waterhen seems much better. In Irish it is known as *cearc uisce.*

All sorts

Moorhens feed while swimming or walking and will sometimes snatch food from other birds such as great crested grebes. They eat all sorts of things including spiders, earthworms, crab apples, pondweed leaves and stems, tadpoles and buttercup seeds.

Redheads

When they hatch, baby moorhens have a bare red patch on their heads and depend on their parents for food for about three weeks. They beg for food by moving their tiny, stumpy wings in a rowing action and pushing their red heads upwards, which stimulates their parents to feed them. As they become more able to feed themselves, the red fades.

Continued on P.48

FOCUS ON RIVERS

by Richard Nairn

Holding on

Because of the currents in the water, tiny animals on the river bed have special ways to avoid being washed downstream. Caddis fly larvae make cases out of tiny stones and cement these to boulders. Flatworms, shrimps and water lice mould their bodies to the shape of the rocks. Blackfly larvae spin threads of silken glue to hang on to. Most of the animal life is *under* the stones in the bed of a river. If you lift a stone to look at its inhabitants be sure to replace it in the exact original position.

Hunters on the wing

Dragonflies are among the most specialised predators of the insect world. They can often be seen in summer darting about above the surface of a river or stream catching other flying insects with their spiny legs. With their huge eyes they can spot a victim ten metres away. Dragonflies are among the fastest known fliers of the insect world. They are noisy eaters and the crunching of their jaws can be heard several metres away. Dragonfly larvae or nymphs live underwater on the river bed. They are also fierce predators of water insects, tadpoles and small fish.

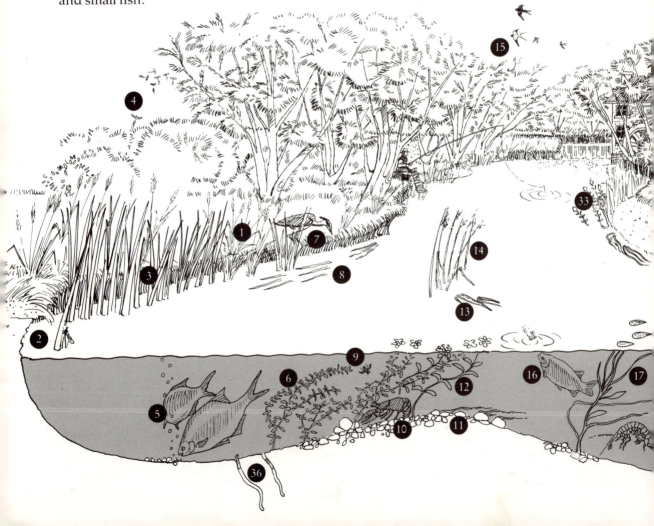

Fishing with a spear

Herons (sometimes known locally as cranes) are common throughout Ireland, feeding in every part of the river from the mountains to the sea. Their long rounded wings measure up to two metres from tip to tip. In flight they fold their long necks back between their shoulders to balance the long legs which they stick straight out behind like a rudder. The usual feeding method for a heron is to stand perfectly still in shallow water for a long time waiting for a fish to swim within reach. Then, like a flash, they strike with the long spear-like bill. Eels are one of their favourite foods, but they will also take frogs and small mammals such as mice and shrews.

Further reading on river wildlife

The book *Irish Rivers* is edited by Éamon de Buitléar and published by Country House.

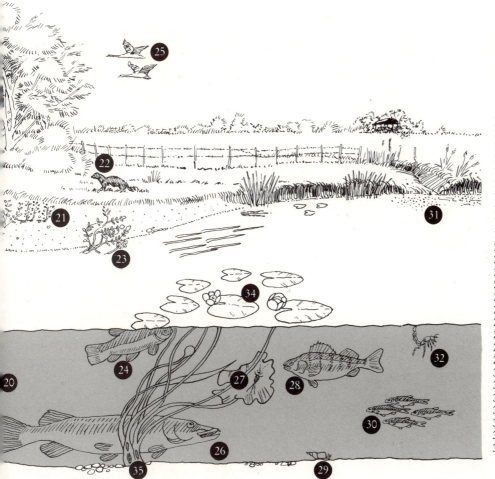

1. canary grass
2. damsel fly
3. bur reed
4. mayfly swarm
5. bream
6. Canadian pondweed
7. heron
8. bur reed floating leaves
9. water boatman
10. crayfish
11. Cladophora alga
12. water starwort
13. clubrush floating leaves
14. clubrush
15. swallow
16. rudd
17. pondweed
18. shrimp
19. ram's horn snail
20. diving beetle
21. water mint
22. mink
23. watercress
24. tench
25. mute swan
26. pike
27. mayfly nymph
28. perch
29. pond snail
30. minnow
31. caddis swarm
32. beetle larva
33. fool's watercress
34. yellow waterlily
35. leech
36. mayfly nymph (*E danica*)

Small Mammal Secrets

by Geoffrey Abbot

You may have read that owls and birds of prey feed on 'small mammals', meaning mice, voles and shrews. But although these secretive creatures are common, we seldom see them. Mice and voles are rodents and have long front teeth adapted for gnawing; while shrews are insectivores and have a large number of sharp, pointed teeth for eating insects and other small animals. Here is a glimpse of Ireland's smallest mammals.

1. **House mice** depend on man and live in or near buildings. A few may breed outside, but they are usually unable to survive for long. They have uniformly grey coloured fur. They are basically grain eaters, but can survive on a wide variety of food, and are pests in houses and factories.

2. **Wood mice**, or **long-tailed field mice**, have strong back legs and feet and move in a series of jumps. Their long tails help them to balance when jumping, and climbing in bushes in search of berries and seeds. Brighter coloured, with larger eyes and ears than house mice. Being nocturnal, they are often eaten by owls.

3. **Bank voles** have rounder noses than wood mice and redder fur. However, they behave very differently; they live in hedges, scrub and woodland and eat seeds, berries and plants, but not grass. They are found only in counties Cork, Kerry, Limerick and Clare.

4. **Pygmy shrews** are smaller than mice or voles and have brown velvety fur that almost hides their small ears. They have tiny eyes and long snouts and feed on insects in all sorts of habitats from woodland to dunes. They make a high-pitched twittery sound.

Turn over part of your compost heap and you may find dozens of worms knotted together at the bottom where it is darkest, wettest and smelliest. Not very nice for us, but perfect for them.

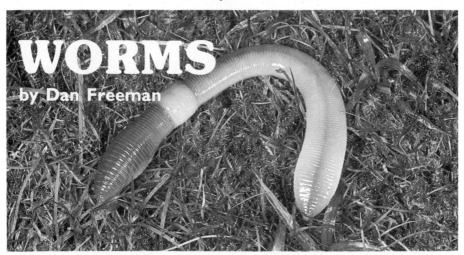

When leaves fall, earthworms and other soil creatures ensure that they decay and the raw materials are returned to the soil to be used again.

In many ways we take these harmless creatures for granted; not realising that we could be lost without them. It was Gilbert White who first discovered facts in favour of the earthworm. His observations in the 18th century revealed that fallen leaves were pulled underground by worms and then used either as burrow-lining or as food. The importance of such an act is enormous, for each leaf contains chemicals which must be released back into the soil as quickly as possible to sustain further plant and animal growth.

The earthworm is one of the most important agents for this vital nutrient re-cycling; and if it seems that there couldn't possibly be enough of them for such an enormous task. . . one hectare of mature grassland may contain three million! Some species pull dead leaves and grasses below the surface, while others come to the surface and leave tell-tale 'worm-casts'.

A single hectare of old grassland – the best place for worms because it is unspoilt and rich in food – may have 30 tonnes of soil passing through its earthworms each year. The burrows resulting from this unseen industry allow water to drain away, allow air to reach underneath the soil and provide vital spaces for roots to penetrate.

But worms have enemies and it is unlikely that the ten years they can live in captivity is ever reached in the wild. If they try to escape above ground they soon fall prey to blackbirds, song thrushes or robins. Their defences are to burrow deeply and quickly when disturbed and to emerge above ground only at night to collect their food when the cool air and damp vegetation stop them drying out. This is when badgers catch them.

Use a torch at night to see worms at work, each with its back end firmly anchored in its burrow entrance, and its front end searching by touch alone. If you stamp your foot, they will pick up the vibration and disappear in a flash. Perhaps it is just as well that only the early bird catches any worms, for without them our world might be little more than a barren wilderness.

(See project on p.18)

Making a
WORMERY

Jim Hurley

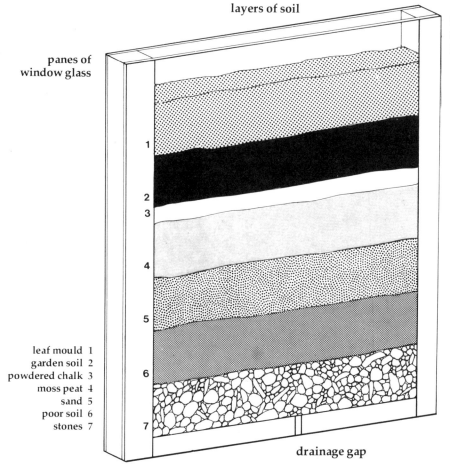

layers of soil

timber lath as
spacer to hold
panes 1cm apart

panes of
window glass

leaf mould 1
garden soil 2
powdered chalk 3
moss peat 4
sand 5
poor soil 6
stones 7

drainage gap

1. Get two identical panes of window glass, each about the size of a large copy-book. Be careful not to rub your fingers along the sharp edges.

2. Get enough pieces of 2cm x 1cm timber lath to go around the sides and bottom of the glass, so as to hold the panes apart. Glue the laths in placed, using a tube of adhesive such as Araldite. Be sure to leave a gap in the base for drainage.

3. Fill the wormery with different layers as shown in the drawing.

4. Water it well. Cover it with a heavy black cloth and prop it up in a safe place with a saucer under the drainage hole.

5. Next day, put in five earthworms and cover the wormery again.

6. Each day take the cover off and study what the worms have been doing. Keep a diary to record what is happening. Make a drawing to show any changes in the layers of soil.

7. There is no need to feed the worms: they will get enough food from the leaf litter. Worms don't live very long in a wormery, so keep the project going for just one week and then empty the wormery and put the worms back where you found them.

BIRD BRAIN
OF IRELAND
Jim Hurley

Birds are clever at solving simple puzzles. Why not test the birds in your garden to see if they can solve the intelligence test shown in the drawing?

You fix the plastic case off a new toothbrush to a board and fill it with peanuts. Salt is bad for birds, so be sure to get peanuts in their shells rather than the salted ones in a packet.

Punch holes in the tube with a scissors and poke matchsticks into the holes, as shown in the drawing, sitting a peanut on each matchstick.

The bird can see the nuts. Do you think it will be able to work out that the way to get a nut to fall into the tray is to pull out a matchstick? Why not set it up in your garden and see how clever your birds are.

For a free leaflet on 'Feeding Wild Birds' send a stamped addressed envelope to the Irish Wildbird Conservancy, Southview, Church Road, Greystones, Co. Wicklow.

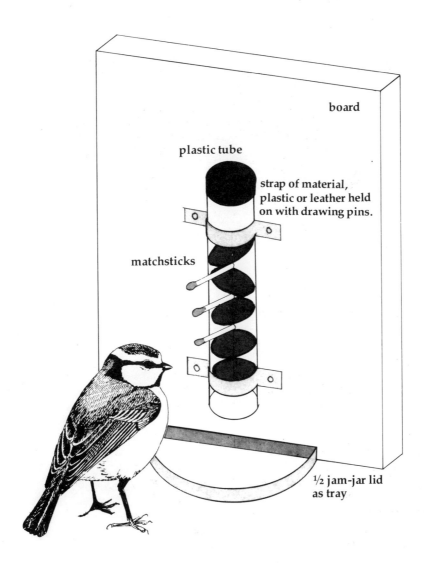

board

plastic tube

strap of material, plastic or leather held on with drawing pins.

matchsticks

½ jam-jar lid as tray

BADGER WATCHING

by Richard Nairn

First find your badgers

Badgers are common mammals in Ireland and make their underground homes (setts) in almost any place where the ground is not too waterlogged. Setts are usually found where there is some cover of trees or bushes but open fields, sand dunes and even gardens are used. Bracken, brambles and nettles often grow thickly around an old sett where the soil has been enriched by the badgers' activities. They usually choose sloping ground to dig into and the tunnels can be many hundreds of metres in length. All the soil and stones are piled outside the entrances to form enormous heaps.

Is the sett active?

Fresh badger footprints in the soil outside an entrance show recent activity. At certain times in the year the badgers clean out their setts and bring to the surface piles of dried grass which they have used for bedding. At an active sett there will be a number of well used and trampled pathways leading away from the entrances in different directions. If you follow several of these pathways you should find some small pits in the ground where the badgers leave their droppings every night. Badgers are very clean animals and fresh droppings are a sure sign of an active sett.

When to go

Normally badgers only come above ground after dark. They emerge from the sett entrances about one hour after sunset. As the days become longer in summer badgers may be active before dark so then you need to take up a watching position at least an hour before sunset. From March to May is a good time of year to watch badgers because the leaves are not yet on the trees and bushes and you can get a much clearer view of what is happening. Clear moonlit nights are the best for visibility.

What to bring

Wear plenty of warm clothes and gloves as nights can be cold! Dark clothing is better and a hood will help to hide your face from reflection in the moonlight. Bring a snack, for you may have a long wait. A pocket torch is useful for checking the time – and finding your way home!

At the sett

Approach very quietly. Always test the wind direction before approaching. (Wet your finger and hold it above your head to feel the direction of light breezes.) Badgers have an excellent sense of smell so position yourself on the downwind side of the sett. The wind should be blowing from the sett to you – not the reverse! Find a shady spot about five metres from the nearest entrance and keep still.

The action begins

Before emerging, badgers always test the air for smells of danger. A black and white nose will appear at the entrance and spend a while sniffing till the 'all clear' signal is given. The adults usually emerge first and have a good scratch after the day spent underground. If there are cubs in this family they will probably play around at the entrance to the sett for a while. Then the whole group will head off along one of the pathways in search of food. Earthworms are high on their list of favourite foods. You can find the holes where badgers have been digging for them all along the pathways.

Be patient

If you don't see the badgers on your first attempt don't be too disappointed. They are sensitive animals and the slightest disturbance or smell of danger may prevent them from coming above ground for the whole night. Try again another night and your patience will be rewarded. Badgers are among the largest of our wild mammals and their behaviour can be fascinating to observe.

Badgers always test the air for smells of danger.

SPRING & SUMMER BOTHER

Thistle

Ragwort

by Rudolf Freund

Sniffle, sniffle, Ah—choo! Watery eyes. Runny nose. If you've ever had these in spring or summer, you may have had hay fever.

Hay fever is an odd name for this misery. It isn't a fever at all but a special chemical irritation of the eyes and nose called an allergy. It isn't caused by hay but by the protein in pollen. When people have an allergy to tiny pollen grains floating in the air their bodies react: *Sniffle, sniffle, ah-choo!*

What is this backyard bother, pollen? Pollen grains are the tiny yellow specks of dust you see inside most flowers. Under a microscope each pollen grain has a special shape. Some are smooth and round. Others are covered with wrinkles, spines or knobs. In any one kind of plant all the pollen grains look alike.

Pollen grows in little sacs in the anthers of a flower. The anthers are the male organs of the plant. For seeds to form, the pollen must reach the stigma, or female part of a flower. When the pollen from an anther is deposited on a stigma, the flower is pollinated.

As plants can't walk around, they need help pollinating their flowers. Something else must move the pollen from the anthers to the stigmas. Often honeybees or hummingbirds looking for nectar will carry pollen dust from flower to flower. The showy colours, nectar and sweet

22

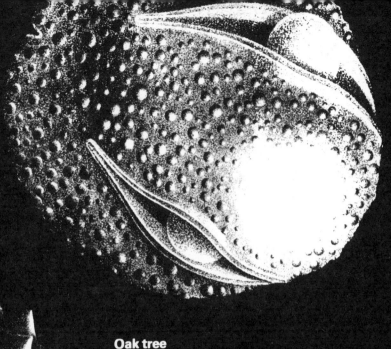

Oak tree

Stigma
Anther
Petal
Ovary

Pollen forms in the anthers and pollinates a flower when it reaches a stigma. Seeds grow in the ovary.

Pictures of the moon? No, these are three kinds of pollen grains, magnified 5000 times.

Pollen can blow a long way. It has been found over 5 kilometres (3mi.) up in the the air and over 100 kilometres across; over 200 pollen grains could fit on the head of a pin! Isn't it amazing that one such tiny pollen grain ever reaches a stigma at all?

A single birch catkin can produce over 10 million pollen grains. And there are hundreds of catkins on a single tree! No wonder great clouds of pollen often float about in the air when trees and shrubs are in flower. Sometimes you can even see a thin yellow layer on the surface of ponds and puddles, or you might sweep yellow dust from your porch.

perfume of many flowers attract insects and birds for this purpose.

Many other plants are pollinated by the wind. These plants — the grasses and many trees — have dull, odourless flowers. But they make lots and lots of tiny, light pollen grains.

With a bit of luck a few of these grains will land on the large, feathery stigma of another flower of its kind. But meanwhile millions of other pollen grains are floating about in the air. Some of this pollen causes the pesky hay fever!

Many people get hay fever when oaks, maples and elms are in flower. Hay fever can make some people quite ill.

When you are miserable and sneezing with hay fever, it's hard to *like* pollen. But without pollen there would be no seeds from which new plants could grow for food and shelter. Without pollen, people and wildlife couldn't exist.

Since plants have to make pollen, doctors are finding ways to help people who suffer from hay fever.

23

caterpillars

Butterflies and moths lay eggs which hatch out into caterpillars. Caterpillars spend most of their time eating. They grow, but their skin doesn't, so they have to change skins (like a snake) three or four times until they are full size. Then the caterpillar changes into a pupa – we usually call it a chrysalis – which changes about inside in a mysterious way (called matamorphosis), until it comes out as a butterfly or moth! This cycle happens every year. There are millions of caterpillars but far fewer adult insects. Why? Because most caterpillars get eaten before they are fully grown.

High energy food
Caterpillars are full of protein and especially good food for young, growing birds. Even some seed eaters, like chaffinches, feed caterpillars to their chicks. A pair of great tits finds about 700 caterpillars every day to feed their young.

Staying alive
Being the best thing on the menu, caterpillars need a few tricks to stay alive. The commonest is simply to try to avoid being seen. Camouflage usually means that they are green, like the leaves they feed on, but some look more like twigs. Others are covered in spiny hairs which irritate birds and make the caterpillar distasteful. Another method is to be brightly coloured, to warn birds that they taste nasty. Most birds seem to avoid these caterpillars without having to learn how they taste for themselves.

Hairy stomachs
Cuckoos are special caterpillar-eaters. They can feed on hairy and brightly-coloured caterpillars which other birds leave alone.

Pulling a face
The puss moth caterpillar is bright green with purple marks to help break up its outline while it feeds on leaves. So birds can't often find it. If, by chance, it is found, the caterpillar rears up and pushes out its frightening face, and lashes out with long red threads from its tail. If even this performance fails, it can squirt strong acid at the bird from a gland in its middle. It is a pretty violent caterpillar!

Safety in numbers

Peacock butterfly caterpillars feed together in colonies on nettle leaves. They are black and covered in spiny hairs. They also spin a silky web for extra protection. Most birds will not eat them, but cuckoos can deal with the hairs and eat whole colonies.

Rugby jerseys

Cinnabar moth caterpillars are brightly patterned in yellow and black hoops. They feed on ragwort leaves and the colours act as a warning to birds not to eat them because they taste horrible. Wasps have the same colours to warn that they sting.

Blending in

Many caterpillars have colours which blend in with the background. As most will only feed on one type of plant, it is not difficult to get the right colour. The green oak tortrix moth has green caterpillars which feed on oak leaves in April and June. They roll the leaf around themselves, but if knocked off can dangle on a tiny thread. Millions can sometimes strip the leaves off whole trees. Birds such as tits and warblers, which have their young just at the time when most caterpillars are about, eat huge numbers.

The **mullein moth** caterpillar lets birds know that it tastes nasty by its colours. It may eat whole flower shoots of mullein plants.

Left
Bright colours and bushy hairs keep birds off **vapourer moth** caterpillars

The **puss moth** caterpillar is a fearsome sight to a small bird. Look for it on willows and poplars.

Far left
The bright colours of **cinnabar moth** caterpillars must make them easy for cuckoos to find. But they warn other birds away.

Spiky hairs are a defence against most birds for the **peacock butterfly** larva, but cuckoos eat a lot of them.

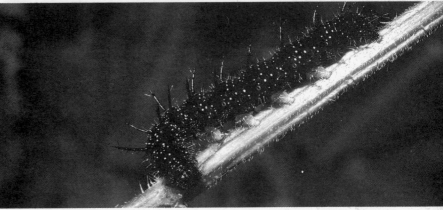

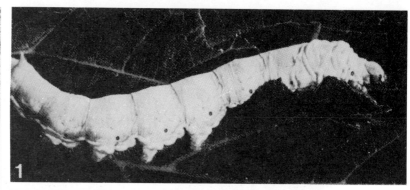

SILK SPINNERS

by Julia Fellows

A beautiful silk kimono. If you lived in Japan, that's what you would wear as your best clothes. Would you guess that this bright, pink fabric came from pale caterpillars called silkworms?

When a silkworm egg hatches, the larva starts eating right away. Silkworms eat only the leaves of mulberry trees. The larva, or caterpillar, eats day and night, stopping only to shed its skin. It grows so much that it outgrows its skin four times.

In 40 days it has grown from a tiny, dark, bristly caterpillar to a large, smooth, creamy white one.[1]

Inside its body are two long silk glands. When the glands are filled with fluid, the caterpillar searches for a safe place. Perhaps it crawls onto a twig.

Then the caterpillar spins its silk. It squeezes the fluid out of its glands through an opening in its lower lip – like squeezing a tiny trail of toothpaste from a tube. The fluid hardens into a shiny thread as it hits the air.

The caterpillar waves its head back and forth in a big figure eight, spinning silk around and around itself. The caterpillar weaves for four days, until all the fluid is used up.

The finished cocoon looks like a wrapped-up peanut.[2] It is made of a single pale yellow strand of silk, sometimes as long as ten football fields end to end.

Inside this silky resting place the silkworm sheds its skin once more. Out of the old caterpillar skin comes a pupa.[3] The pupa is the resting stage before changing to a moth.

If the cocoon is going to be made into silk thread, the pupa is killed by heating it.

Then the silk is unwound from the cocoon, twisted together with silk from other cocoons, dyed, and woven into silk fabric.

But some of the cocoons are allowed to complete the life cycle. Three weeks after the silkworm spins its cocoon, the silk moth breaks the silk wall at one end and pulls itself out.[4]

The new moth looks nothing like the caterpillar! It is furry, white and has wings. Because its wings are small, the silk moth cannot fly. As a caterpillar, it ate all the time. The moth does not eat at all.

Once out of its cocoon, the silk moth looks for a mate. When a male finds a female, it whirs its wings rapidly in a courtship dance. Then the male clasps the abdomen of the female and they

mate.[5] In a few days the male dies.

After mating the female begins to lay eggs.[6] She lays about 500, then dies. Soon the eggs will hatch, and new caterpillars will spin their silky cocoons.

27

THE IRISH STOAT

Raymond Piper

by Patrick Sleeman

There is a fierce little animal which lives by hunting other animals and is found all over Ireland. It has sharp teeth and a long thin body so that it can hunt and kill its victims wherever they might hide. This animal is the Irish stoat, which is often mistakenly called a weasel.

Special fur coat

We know it is a stoat because it has a black tip to its tail, something weasels never have. There are no weasels in Ireland. The Irish stoat has a dark brown coat and white belly. The line between the white and brown is wavy. This squiggly line is peculiar to the Irish stoat and makes it different from stoats found anywhere else. It is because of this that we think that stoats were one of the very first animals to arrive in Ireland. Having been here so long they have become a separate race.

Stoats are one of the most common hunting animals. They are found all over the world, except in very hot countries. In very cold countries like Russia, the stoats turn white in winter, all except for the black tail tip. A white stoat is called an ermine. Ermine fur is one of the most valuable and sought-after furs in the world. Such fur is often used in costumes of kings and queens. The Irish stoat does not turn white in winter.

Frightened to death

Stoats are well known for their ability to kill animals bigger than themselves. For example they regularly kill rabbits which are often much larger. A stoat will select and hunt a single rabbit, ignoring all others in its path. The victims often give up hope and sit squealing with terror awaiting their end. Examination of rabbits which have been hunted and apparently killed by stoats often reveals that the rabbit died not of any bodily injury but simply of fright.

Stoats also kill rats and mice, being able to follow them down their tunnels. Often a stoat will take over a rat's nest, which is just the right size. A stoat will sometimes line its den with the skins of rats and mice that it has killed and eaten. Stoats also climb trees where they will raid birds' nests and they will use such nests as dens. Again the stoat's size and shape allow it to climb freely and enter small nest chambers and devour the unfortunate inhabitants. Stoats kill their victims quickly,

28

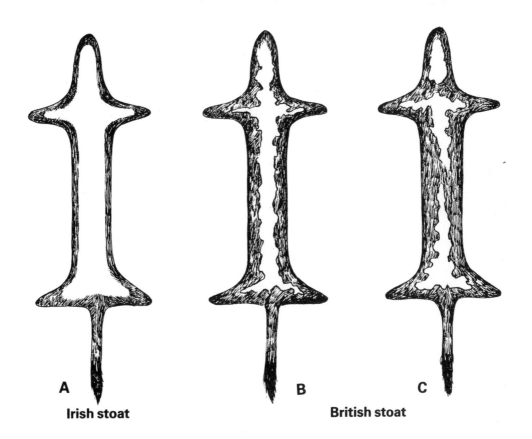

A
Irish stoat

B

C

British stoat

usually by biting them at the base of the head and breaking the neck. However when killing adult birds they are known to bite at the base of the wings, which prevents the bird from flying.

Undercover operator

People don't often see stoats, despite the fact that they are very common. This is because they are good at using cover and only rarely travel over open areas such as a field. They can sometimes be seen crossing roads. They are also found when hunting rabbits because the squeal of the doomed rabbit may give the stoat away. Should you come across a freshly killed rabbit wait very quietly and the stoat may reappear to repossess its victim. Stoats appear to be wary of venturing into the open due to an instinctive fear of birds of prey, like hawks and owls. These birds could easily catch them away from cover. When a stoat is chased like this in the open it will swish its black-tipped tail. This is known to distract the bird and sometimes allows the stoat to escape. Dogs, cats, otters, pine martens and foxes will also kill stoats, but may not eat them.

A family of stoats can be as many as twelve young. This large litter size makes sure that the stoats that get killed every year are replaced. In Ireland the young are born about the beginning of April, usually in a converted rat's nest. The mother will suckle the young in the nest for some time, but soon they move onto solid food and they will learn to hunt from their mother. Most stoats live for about a year. As agile and adaptable hunters they play an important role in the Irish countryside.

FIRST AID FOR WILD BIRDS

Did you ever find a wild bird by the side of the road – hit by a passing car but still alive? Did your cat ever bring in a small bird dazed but not too badly hurt? Casualties such as this have a chance of survival and they may need just a little care and feeding to help them return to the wild.

First, a word of warning

In summertime, lots of young wild birds leave their nests and take their first flight. This usually results in a bumpy landing in an unsuitable place such as the middle of a lawn. Fledglings such as this are *not* lost, orphaned or abandoned. If left alone, the parent birds will continue to feed the young one and will lead it out of danger. If there are cats or other predators about move the young bird under cover of a thick bush or hedge and then LEAVE IT ALONE.

Catching and handling a bird

Catching an injured or sick bird is often difficult and may result in further injury to the bird if care is not taken. Most birds become quieter in the dark so throwing a sheet over the casualty may help. Hold the bird loosely but keeping its wings close to the body to prevent flapping. Larger birds such as ducks or seabirds should be lifted with two hands, one holding each wing close against the body. Never hold a bird near your face as the beak is a sharp weapon and could injure your eyes.

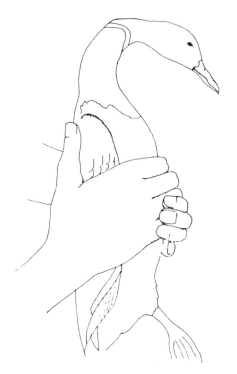

A method of holding a large bird, with the wings folded against its side.

Find out what is wrong

A bird which has lost a lot of blood should be given liquid such as glucose solution. Hold the beak open, tilt the head back and put in a few drops at a time with an eye dropper. Injured birds with broken wings or legs should always be taken to a vet for expert treatment. If the bird appears to be suffering from shock it should be left in a dark box with plenty of air holes for several hours. If it is cold or wet it may require some heat so the airing cupboard is a good place to put the box.

Where to keep a bird

Small birds may be kept in a bird cage if this has been well disinfected before use. Such cages should be covered with a dark cloth to prevent the bird flying at the wire and damaging itself. A perch at least ten centimetres from the floor of the cage should be provided. Larger birds should be kept out of doors in a larger cage at least one metre square and covered with fine wire mesh. Make a roof over the cage to shelter the bird from rain. Remember to make the cage secure from cats!

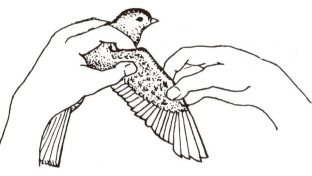

Examination of a bird's wing

What kind of food to give
Different types of birds require different foods. Finches, buntings and sparrows mainly prefer seeds. Robins, blackbirds and thrushes mainly eat animal food such as insects. They may be offered dead flies, chopped worms or caterpillars. A packet of dried insect food used for fish tanks could be bought in a pet shop if you cannot find any natural food. Seabirds prefer oily fish such as mackerel or herring cut into thin finger-sized strips. Most ducks, geese and swans will eat grain such as wheat or oat flakes soaked in water to soften them.

If the bird will not eat
Try offering the food in different ways – in a container, scattered on the ground or hanging from the side of the cage. Offer a choice of foods and leave the bird alone to eat it. You may have to force the bird to eat if it is starving. Holding the head back and the beak open drop very small quantities of food down the throat to avoid choking. If the bird will not swallow, use a plastic syringe to squirt some water down the throat. All birds should be given a container of water for drinking and bathing.

Other problems need expert help
Birds suffering from poisoning or oil pollution require special treatment. Great care should be taken in handling such birds. Contact your local vet and ask advice in dealing with seriously injured birds.

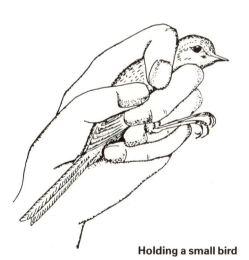

Holding a small bird

Return to the wild
The main aim of caring for a wild bird is to help it recover so that it can return to the wild. It should be released as early as possible at or near the spot where it was found. Ideally, the release site should be well away from human disturbance.

Free leaflet
If you would like a free leaflet with further information on 'First Aid for Wild Birds' send a stamped addressed envelope with 'First Aid Leaflet' in the top left-hand corner to IWC, Southview, Church Road, Greystones, Co. Wicklow.

Making a
NEST BOX

by Richard Nairn

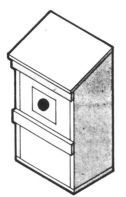

House martin box

Some birds need holes and crevices in which to nest. But very few old trees survive long enough in gardens to provide suitable nesting places. You can help to make up for this shortage by putting up nest boxes.

Which are the commonest nestbox users?

Blue tits and great tits will nest in almost any shape of box provided that it has the correct size entrance hole. This should not be larger than 28 millimetres in diameter (about the size of a ten pence coin) or house sparrows may take over. If half of the front is left open robins, pied wagtails and spotted flycatchers may use the box for nesting.

Where should the box be placed?

Ideally the box should be fixed to a sturdy tree at least three metres from the ground. If there is no tree available the outside wall of a house or shed would be suitable especially if you can grow a creeper on the wall to provide some foliage. The box should preferably be facing either north or east to avoid both the hot sun and the wetter winds.

Hole-nesting box

When should the box be put up?

Birds will begin to investigate the box in late winter but nest building will not begin before March or April. Ideally the box should be in position by New Year so that the birds are used to it well before nesting begins. They may use it for overnight roosting during cold winter periods. Old nests may be removed from the box in winter to leave space for the following spring. Do not use insecticides or flea powders in the box as these are harmful to the birds.

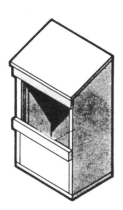

How do you know if birds are nesting?

It is not a good idea to look in the box more often than every two weeks as the birds may easily desert it if there is too much disturbance. If you see a bird entering and leaving the box carrying nesting material such as grass, straw and feathers then you can be sure it is building a nest. After egg laying there will be a quiet period of about three weeks while the birds are incubating (sitting on the eggs). When you see the adults making regular visits carrying food such as caterpillars it will be feeding the young nestlings. Within a further three weeks the young birds will make their first flights.

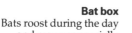

Open-fronted nestbox

Bat box

Bats roost during the day and may use specially constructed boxes. Made from rough sawn timber, it is similar to a hole-nesting box, but has a one centimetre entrance at the base and a grooved back to which bats may cling.

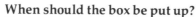

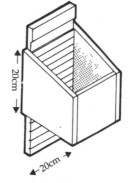

20cm

20cm

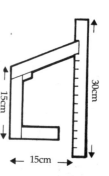

15cm

30cm

15cm

water. Sprats are small, herring-like fish, up to about 16cm long. Like sand-eels, they are often found in large shoals. Puffins, razorbills and guillemots dive into them from the surface of the sea. Razorbills use their wings and feet to swim after their prey, but guillemots and puffins use only their wings. Both sand-eels and sprats are used for making into fish-meal (used as fertiliser and animal food) and many are now caught by trawlers. Because of this there is a danger that not enough will be left for the birds.

Mackerel

Mackerels spend the winter at the bottom of the sea. During spring they move to shallow coastal waters to spawn, then form small feeding shoals. They return to deep water in autumn. During their breeding season, gannets feed on these mackerel shoals by diving from as high as 30m. The gannet spots its prey before it plunges, watching it on its way down and hitting the water at up to 60 mph. The fish is caught in its bill and usually swallowed underwater.

Flounder

Flounders are bottom-living flat-fish and because of this they have both their eyes on the same side of their body – usually on the right. They hide by burying themselves in mud, but cormorants still find many after diving from the surface. They catch them in their bill and bring the fish to the surface to eat.

Minnow and stickleback

Minnows and sticklebacks are the main food of the kingfisher. The kingfisher waits on a branch above the water. When a suitable fish swims by, the kingfisher dives on it, grasping it in its bill and returning to its perch, before swallowing its prey, head first.

See *The Hamlyn Guide to Freshwater Fishes of Britain and Europe* by Dr P S Maitland.

Left
Sand-eels are small,
eel-like fish up to 20cm
long. They are the
main food of terns.

33

A JAM-JAR AQUARIUM

Jim Hurley

Project 3

Many people think of an aquarium as a place to keep large creatures like fish or tadpoles, but the aim of this project is to study tiny creatures instead.

1. Scrub an old jam-jar or coffee-jar until it is perfectly clean and rinse it well.

2. Quarter-fill it with mud from the bed of a pond, canal, lake or quiet backwater of a river. (Take a friend along, just in case you fall in and need rescuing.)

3. Now fill it up with pond water (that friend will come in useful again) and allow it to stand for several days until the water clears. Keep the lid off. Once the water has cleared do not move the jar again.

4. Draw the creatures that you see and write notes about what they are doing.

Flatworms glide across the mud. They can also crawl upsidedown on the surface film.

Water mites are fat and are brightly coloured.

The **leech** can swim as well as crawl. It preys on snails and worms.

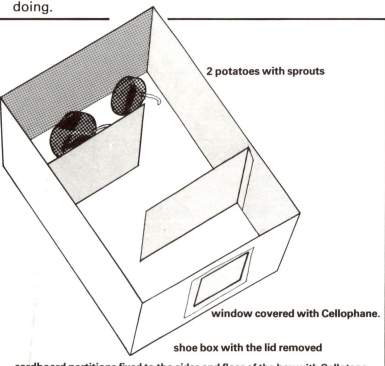

2 potatoes with sprouts

window covered with Cellophane.

shoe box with the lid removed

cardboard partitions fixed to the sides and floor of the box with Sellotape. These partitions extend three-quarters-way across the box.

POTATOES ON THE MOVE

Project 4

Plants move rather slowly, but they do move about. One of the things that causes them to move is light. You can study this by trying this experiment.

Set up the experiment as shown in the diagram. Cover the box with the lid and thick, dark cloth and put it in a warm place with good light shining in the window. Leave it alone for about three weeks. Write a short account of what has happened.

34

JAM-JAR AQUARIUM
Animal Life Illustrated

Freshwater shrimps swim backwards.

The **water flea** swims in a jerky fashion.

This is a copepod called **cyclops**. It is a female with two bulging egg-sacs.

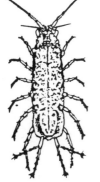

The **water louse** crawls around slowly.

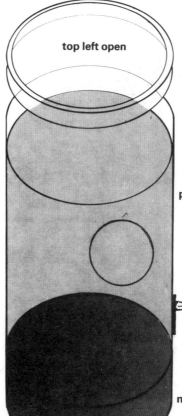

top left open

pond water

mud

The **blood worm** lives with its head in the mud. Its tail sticks up vertically in the water and waves from side to side.

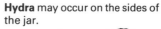

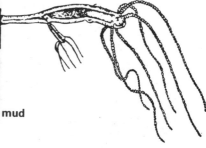

Hydra may occur on the sides of the jar.

The body of the **ostracod** is covered by a shell. It is a poor swimmer so it skips along the surface of the mud.

The **pea-shell cockle** hides under the mud.

ENDANGERED...

by Sylvia Sullivan

Passenger pigeon

EXTINCT

Have you heard the saying, as dead as a dodo? The dodo was a large, flightless bird which lived on Mauritius, an island in the Indian Ocean. It became extinct in the 17th century, when the island was colonised by the Dutch, because it was unable to cope with the sudden appearance of man, and the other predators – cats, rats, dogs and pigs – which arrived with him.

Of course, some birds are able to adapt more easily than others when conditions change. But in the last few hundred years an increasing number of species have become extinct because of man's activities. Man has hunted hundreds of animals to extinction for food, like the passenger pigeon and the great auk. He has destroyed others because they were a nuisance to him, or because he introduced new predators such as rats. Other species have suffered from pollution, e.g. pesticides and oil.

The greatest threat of all is loss of habitat such as the destruction of tropical forests, the drainage of wetlands to provide more agricultural land or the destruction of bogland by conifer planting. Today, conservationists are taking desperate measures to save some of the world's endangered birds. Each species has its own, special needs which have to be considered.

Golden-shouldered parrot

ENDANGERED

EXTINCT

Dodo

Some members of the parrot family are known to be very rare. The reasons for this are not always clear. The brightly-coloured grass parrots of Australia are thought to have been badly affected by habitat changes caused by man and by the introduction of starlings which compete with them for nest-holes. Other species, such as the red-tailed parrot of Brazil, and the St Lucia parrot from the West Indies, have declined because their dense forest habitat is being widely destroyed. Many parrots are still hunted for their feathers and there is no doubt that extra pressure is put on them by collectors who export them as cage birds.

Captive breeding is used very much as a last resort, and will only work for some species. It is being tried for the Japanese crested ibis, now reduced to less than ten birds.

Both the Laysan duck and the Hawaiian goose have recovered from the brink of extinction, as a result of captive breeding. However, these last ditch efforts are not good enough. Prevention is better than cure, and we must preserve the habitats that support whole communities of wildlife. If the places where animals and plants live disappear, there can be no hope for them in the long-term.

crested Ibis

ENDANGERED

THE ROBIN FAMILY

by Elizabeth Fritz

Mr and Mrs Robin were building a nest. For several days they had been flying to a branch halfway up our pear tree. As they flew, wisps of material dangled from their beaks.

From our porch we could see the nest taking shape. It couldn't have been more than 12 centimetres (about 5 inches) in diametre.

Mrs Robin wove coarse grass, twigs, bits of paper, cloth and string to make the base and sides. Next she brought moss in her bill from our garden wall where snow still lay in patches. She placed the moss on the inside of the woven nest. Then she plopped down in the mossy nest and wiggled around and around, pressing the moss against the sides

with her breast and wings. When the weaving job was done she lined the cup-shaped nest with soft grasses and downy feathers.

The nest building took three days. Sometimes Mr Robin perched up high on a telephone wire and trilled to warn all other robins that they had better stay out of his territory. He didn't mind trespassing sparrows or thrushes – but he would puff out his red breast and peck at other robins.

One night we heard the wind roaring through the pear tree. Would the nest be blown out? The next morning it was still there, and Mrs Robin had settled in. We could see her tail sticking up like a flag.

Day after day Mr Robin came to bring her food. Once we saw him astride the nest, guarding it while she had a little outing. By craning our necks we could see four blue eggs.

About two weeks later we awoke one morning to see Mr and Mrs Robin flying around with pieces of blue eggshell in their beaks. The babies had broken out of the shells, and the parents were cleaning house.

We could see four big yellow beaks and the bright orange insides of four hungry mouths popping up from the nest. Mr and Mrs Robin pulled juicy earthworms from the ground. Between the two of them they fed the babies worms and insects at least 50 times a day.

By the end of two weeks the naked, squirmy babies had grown tan and brown feathers, and had speckled breasts. The babies were now so big they overflowed the nest. When they slept their heads hung down over the edge. They pushed and shoved each other, trying to stretch their wings.

Finally one of the babies climbed out of the cramped quarters. We could barely see him on the branch close to the nest. His speckled breast acted as camouflage. He made a move to get back in, but the other babies cheeped a clear and noisy 'No!' Slowly Number One inched his way along the branch. Before he had gone very far, Number Two stood up on the edge of the nest and stepped onto the branch. As he moved away, Numbers Three and Four followed.

By this time we had lost track of Number One. Then we saw Mrs Robin standing on the ground below the tree, a grasshopper in her mouth. Number One flapped his wings and fluttered to the ground – and she gave him the grasshopper as a reward.

Continued on P.64

Number One baby inched bravely along the branch. Number Two soon followed.

what's in your

In winter, when natural food is in short supply, a great variety of wild birds may visit your garden in search of scraps. Putting food out regularly may help them survive and will give you lots of pleasure. This guide will help you identify the common birds and a few unusual winter visitors.

Magpie – large black and white crow. Common in gardens in some areas.

Blackcap – greyish/brown, sparrow-sized bird. Male has black cap, female has brown cap. Unusual visitor.

Bullfinch – shy, plump bird with short, thick bill. White rump shows in flight.

Male

Redwing – white stripe over eye and under cheek, red flanks. Less common winter visitor.

Female

Wren – secretive, tiny bird with upright tail. Sings in winter. Fairly common.

garden?

Sparrowhawk – fast-flying with broad, blunt wings. Collared dove size. Unusual visitor, swooping onto garden birds.

Starling – slightly smaller than a blackbird. Noisy and aggressive. Very common.

Robin – unmistakable, visits most gardens.

Chaffinch – white on tail and wings in both sexes. Female duller than male. Common.

House sparrow – male is more colourful than female and has black bib. Noisy and common.

Song thrush – warm brown above, spotted below. Alert looking. Hops or runs. Common.

Dunnock – creeps along ground. Usually keeps close to cover. Fairly common.

Blackbird – male black, female brown. Bold and common in gardens.

41

Continued on P.65

ON THE ANIMAL TRAIL
Signs to look out for

by Éamon de Buitléar

Tracking animals can be fun, even if you think that you are not very good at it. If you use a bit of imagination you can make up stories about who meets what and even where a particular animal went after you have lost its trail. The easy tracks to follow are those ones left in mud, sand or snow and if you want to build up a collection of footprints, these are ideal for plaster casts. But there are lots of other signs too which can tell us what has been going on in our neighbourhood.

Many animals move around after dark because this is the time they feel safest. Very often the food they are after comes out at night too. Badgers, for example, love earthworms and they find plenty of these around during the hours of darkness. Probably the best known of these night wanderers is the hedgehog and a pretty noisy visitor it can be too as it snuffles and snorts around the garden. Last autumn I heard quite a racket outside my back door where something or someone was obviously pulling the cat's dish around the place. I carefully opened the door and there under the window were four hedgehogs having a tussle over the remains of the cat's dinner! Whether they sensed me or heard some other sounds coming from the house, the whole spiky family scuttled off down the garden and were lost to the darkness. If you find long black droppings showing the remains of shiny beetles and other insects, you will know that the hedgehogs have been at work. Hedgehogs eat slugs and snails too, so they are the welcome friends of gardeners.

Snails are also a favourite food of the song thrush and a scattering of broken snail shells will tell you where the thrush has been at work. Before the bird eats the snail it removes the shell by banging it and smashing it against a stone. This stone is called the thrush's anvil. If you watch this area you will see how the thrush works like a blacksmith, hammering away at its anvil!

The snails that are lucky enough to escape the hedgehog and the thrush move around the garden much more easily in damp conditions. After a good night's fall of dew you will find their silvery trails all over the garden. A hot, dry day is not at all suitable for laying down a shiny trail, so when conditions are too dry the snail quits work and waits for the evening dew, or for a nice heavy shower, before going out for a slide!

When I recently found a small pile of hazelnuts near a tree trunk, it did not take long to find out who had collected them. There was a small hole in each nut with tiny tooth-marks radiating on the inside of each one. Now what small animals would have been feeding here, you might ask?

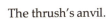
The thrush's anvil.

The remains of the meal were beside a small burrow where some of the nuts had been pulled inside. A small mammal with sharp teeth, yes! – surely a woodmouse, or longtailed field mouse, which is its other name. Sometimes you may find the woodmouse's home in a shed, but it prefers to live in a hedgerow where it has its nest in a small underground hole. If you grow peas in your garden, you may be sure that the woodmouse will be delighted at finding such a nice row of countless tasty dinners!

While you are looking around the garden, have you noticed that some of the rose bushes have had semi-circular pieces cut from the leaves? This is the work of the leaf-cutter bee. Keep an eye out for this interesting insect and you will see how skilfully it carves the leaf with its jaws. It is the female bee which carries out this work and as she folds the piece of leaf neatly under her body, she then flies off with it to her nest. This may be in a cavity in a wooden board or in a stack of flower pots. I have even found them nesting in the rotting wooden beams of an old glasshouse.

But back to tracks! If you find the fresh signs of an animal in a particular place you may be already on the way to getting a good view of your subject and your next step is to find your quarry.

If you are planning to watch animals at night you could try using a piece of red cellophane fixed to the front of your flash lamp. Animals do not seem to see the red light and you can even get quite close to hedgehogs as they hunt around your garden at night.

Whatever time of day or night you choose to watch animals, remember that it requires a great deal of patience. You will have to spend long periods sitting still and remaining absolutely quiet and the longer you watch the more you should learn. Animals have much keener noses and ears than we have, so keep the wind in your direction and try to move as silently as possible. Good hunting!

CURIOUS
CUCKOOS

by Chris Harbard

A fledgling cuckoo will demand food from any passing bird, using a loud, begging call. The willow warbler is rarely used as a host – this one may have been carrying food to its own young when it was attracted by the calling cuckoo.

There are many stories and myths about the cuckoo that stem from its strange breeding behaviour, which we still do not clearly understand.

Many people who listen for the well-known calls each spring, never see one of these slim, long-tailed, grey birds. Cuckoos spend the winter in Africa and migrate north across the Sahara Desert to Europe, normally arriving in Ireland in the middle of April. Because they arrive at the same time as April showers, hearing one is said to be a sign of rain and from this many other superstitions have

grown linking cuckoos with good or bad luck.

It is the male bird that makes the familiar 'cuck-oo' call to advertise its territory. Sometimes this changes to 'cuck-cuck-oo', usually during courtship. The call of the female is a less well known, clear bubbling sound, given particularly after egg-laying.

The cuckoo is a 'brood-parasite', a bird that lays its eggs in the nests of other 'host'

Below
Cuckoos look like sparrowhawks and young cuckoos even have a white patch on the back of the neck like these birds of prey. This may help to protect them from attack.

species instead of building its own. The foster parents incubate and bring up the young cuckoo instead of their own brood. Many birds in other countries adopt this method of breeding, including a South American duck! The female cuckoo watches carefully to find possible foster parents building a nest. She then flies to the nest, removes an egg, lays one of her own in its place and flies off with the host's egg in her bill and eats it. One female will lay between 10 and 20 eggs in a season.

An individual female will always lay eggs of the same colour to imitate those of the species she usually uses. A cuckoo's egg in a robin's nest looks different from one in a pied wagtail's nest. This egg matching helps to ensure that the host does not notice the new egg and either push it out or desert the nest.

Continued on P.77

Below
Cuckoo eggs laid in dunnock nests do not look like the blue eggs of the host – but dunnocks do not seem able to tell the difference.

Left
A newly hatched cuckoo ejects the eggs from a warbler's nest.

WILDLIFE QUIZ

Jim Hurley

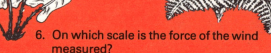

Test yourself or your friends. See how many of these questions you can get right.

Answers on page 74

1. What is a baby goose called?
2. What is an elver?
3. What is a hare's resting place called?
4. Name the green substance found in the leaves of plants.
5. The red admiral, peacock and small tortoiseshell butterflies lay eggs on the same plant. Name the plant.

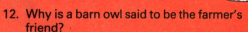

6. On which scale is the force of the wind measured?
7. What are red, sika and fallow?
8. What is a vixen?
9. Where do cuckoos build their nests?
10. What is a baby swan called?
11. What is the name of a badger's breeding place?

12. Why is a barn owl said to be the farmer's friend?
13. Can you eat oak apples?
14. What are hart's tongue and rusty back?
15. Which insect lives as an adult for only a few hours?
16. Does a female robin have a red breast like the male?
17. Where are real pearls found?
18. What is made from flax?
19. What is a thrush's anvil?
20. Name a mammal that flies.

21. Does the moon give off its own light?
22. Why do kestrels hover?
23. What are brent, barnacle and white-front?
24. Which crab lives in an empty seashell?
25. What is a mermaid's purse?
26. Name the largest Irish seabird.
27. Which is the smallest Irish mammal?
28. Name a bird that eats and even sleeps on the wing?
29. Which is the largest Irish mammal?
30. What is the smallest bird in Ireland?

31. Silverfish live in water: true or false?
32. What is a newt?
33. How many species of bats in Ireland – three, seven, or ten?
34. Do most spiders have four, eight, or twelve eyes?
35. What is a tern?
36. Which creature makes the cuckoo spit?
37. Which species of bird is known as the Irish nightingale?
38. What fish is featured on the ten-pence coin?
39. What is lady's smock?
40. What is a sea heart?

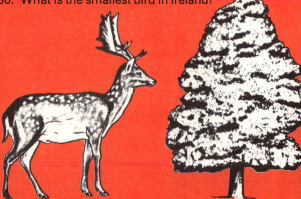

Project 5

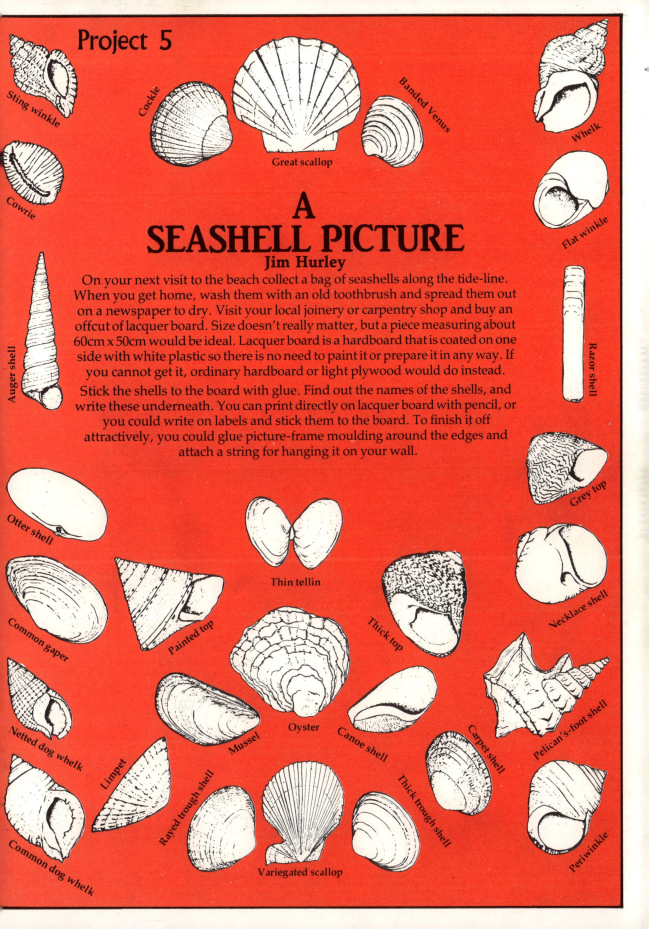

Sting winkle

Cockle

Great scallop

Banded Venus

Whelk

Cowrie

Flat winkle

Auger shell

Razor shell

A SEASHELL PICTURE
Jim Hurley

On your next visit to the beach collect a bag of seashells along the tide-line. When you get home, wash them with an old toothbrush and spread them out on a newspaper to dry. Visit your local joinery or carpentry shop and buy an offcut of lacquer board. Size doesn't really matter, but a piece measuring about 60cm x 50cm would be ideal. Lacquer board is a hardboard that is coated on one side with white plastic so there is no need to paint it or prepare it in any way. If you cannot get it, ordinary hardboard or light plywood would do instead.

Stick the shells to the board with glue. Find out the names of the shells, and write these underneath. You can print directly on lacquer board with pencil, or you could write on labels and stick them to the board. To finish it off attractively, you could glue picture-frame moulding around the edges and attach a string for hanging it on your wall.

Grey top

Otter shell

Thin tellin

Thick top

Necklace shell

Common gaper

Painted top

Oyster

Canoe shell

Carpet shell

Pelican's-foot shell

Netted dog whelk

Limpet

Mussel

Thick trough shell

Periwinkle

Common dog whelk

Rayed trough shell

Variegated scallop

Showing the colours

The moorhen's red shield is used as a threat to other birds. In winter flocks some birds dominate others. These dominant birds are not the largest in size but those with the largest shield. In courtship the head is lowered to hide the shield.

White patches under the tail are also used in displays. The tail is fanned out to show them off to intruders in a 'hunched display'. When courting a female the male will swim round her with his tail raised to display his white patches.

Right from the start

Coots and moorhens look rather similar at first glance. But coots are larger, rounder birds with white bills and face shields. Moorhens flick their tails which shows off the white feathers underneath. Coots are birds of open, deep water, while moorhens prefer the plant-covered edges or ditches.

Big feet

Although moorhens look very clumsy, their big feet allow them, not only to walk and run quickly, but to swim, perch and climb trees as well! Also their long toes help to spread their weight so that they do not sink on soft mud or floating vegetation. Coots, which spend more time on water, have fleshy lobes on the sides of their toes to help them swim and dive.

coot

moorhen

WINTER TWIGS

You could make a nice collection of winter twigs off trees in the following way.

Collect twigs about 30cm long and about as thick as your finger. Cut them neatly off the tree using a small saw, such as a hacksaw. Never crack or break them off.

At home, trim them all off to the same length and arrange them on a piece of thin board or the side of a large cardboard box. Punch holes in the board on each side of the twigs and tie them on using strong thread or light twine. Keep all the knots to the back of the board. Plastic-covered wire ties, the sort used for freezer bags, are ideal for this job if you have some. Find the name of each tree and label your twigs. You now have a nice display for your wall or your school nature table.

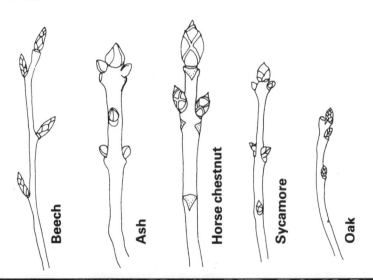

Beech   Ash   Horse chestnut   Sycamore   Oak

SILENT NIGHT HUNTERS
Owls and their prey

by Richard Nairn

A fleeting glimpse in the car headlights is the most common way for people to see owls. The familiar rounded head shows up clearly even in silhouette.

Which owl?

There are only three species of owl which are regularly seen in Ireland. These are the barn owl, the long-eared owl and the short-eared owl. The short-eared owl is mainly a winter visitor and often hunts by day over sand dunes. It is the rarest of the three and has only bred occasionally in Ireland.

The barn owl

Often known as the 'white owl' in Ireland, the barn owl can vary from almost pure white to golden brown. The face and underparts are normally white while the upper parts are usually pale golden-buff with fine speckles. Females are generally darker than males and this may help to camouflage them on the nest.

The long-eared owl

The other resident owl in Ireland is the long-eared owl, so called because of the tufts of feathers on each side of the head. These are not true ears and are sometimes not very obvious as they are laid flat when the owl is in flight. The body feathers are generally mottled brown and buff all over with a much darker appearance than the barn owl.

Silent hunters

All owls are perfectly adapted for silent flight. They are covered with a thick layer of soft feathers which extends even to the legs and feet. The feathers on the front edge of the wing have a special comb-like fringe to silence the wing as it cuts through the air. Silence is important because owls rely on surprise to catch their prey.

Pin-point vision

Unlike most birds which have eyes on opposite sides of the head, owls have binocular vision like humans. Both eyes face forward and are highly accurate in judging distances. The eyes are unusually large for the size of the birds and are very sensitive even in poor light. To help in locating prey, owls can turn the head in any direction without moving the rest of the body.

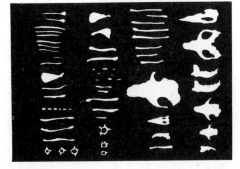

Owl pellet and its contents

Sharp hearing

Just like a radar scanner, the round face of the owl, with its stiff bristly feathers, collects the slightest sounds and focuses them on the large ear openings hidden in the head feathers. So accurate is its hearing that an owl perched on a tall tree can locate a mouse moving in the undergrowth some twenty metres below.

Nest sites

As the name suggests barn owls often nest in deserted farm buildings but ruined castles, hollow trees, cavities in cliffs and even old crows' nests are sometimes used. Long-eared owls are almost always found in woodland where they commonly breed in old nests of hooded crows, magpies, wood pigeons and sparrowhawks. A heap of pellets may often be found below the nesting tree.

Food supply

Small mammals such as mice and rats make up the bulk of the diet for both barn owls and long-eared owls. Field mice are the most common prey but in cities and towns house mice and rats are more plentiful. Occasionally pygmy shrews, small birds, frogs, bats and large insects such as dor beetles are captured. In areas of the south-west, where the bank vole occurs, these introduced mammals also form an important food resource for owls.

Owl pellets

A good way to find out the prey of an owl is to examine the pellets which it coughs up after each meal. These consist of a neat packet of all the bones, feathers, fur and hard parts of insects in the food. Long-eared owl pellets are greyish in colour but those of the barn owls are covered in a shiny black coating. When the pellet is broken open, tiny skulls and jaw bones give clues to the owl's victims.

Hunting grounds

The barn owl prefers to hunt in open country. It will sometimes perch on a fence post before gliding effortlessly across the fields in search of prey. By contrast the long-eared owl usually hunts in woodland or forestry plantations where it has plenty of cover. When the owls are roosting by day the same hunting grounds are used by kestrels and sparrowhawks. Because they fly slowly and close to the ground, owls are often killed by passing cars on the roads.

Shooting and protection

Despite being protected by the law, owls are sometimes shot either through ignorance, fear or simply curiosity. Their night-time activities and haunting calls have made owls the subject of much superstition. The 'wise owl' is supposed by some people to be able to predict disasters. In fact, owls are quite remarkable birds, which can help us by keeping down the populations of rats and mice. They deserve special protection from disturbance.

WHAT'S NEW

Recent news on wildlife conservation
Compiled by Richard Nairn

COTTONWEED CONTROVERSY

The best individual entry in the 1986 Aer Lingus Young Scientist Competition was won by Stephen Langrell of Gorey, Co. Wexford. He studied the conservation needs of a very rare plant called cottonweed which grows on a shingle beach in south County Wexford. This silvery plant with its yellow, daisy-like flowers is not found anywhere else in Ireland or Britain. Its survival depends on the combination of sand and shingle on the beach and it is unable to compete with other wild plants such as grasses. Despite protection by law the plants are being damaged by heavy machinery driving over them and by the removal of beach sand. Unless something is done soon this plant will become extinct in Ireland.

TERNS PROTECTED

One of the rarest seabirds breeding in Ireland is the little tern with less than 300 pairs in the whole country. It is especially vulnerable because it nests on popular sandy beaches where people like to go swimming, fishing, sailing, jogging or simply walking the dog. Terns' eggs look just like pebbles on the sand so they are easily trampled without the people knowing that they have done any harm. In 1986 special watches were set up by the Irish Wildbird Conservancy at a number of little tern colonies in Counties Louth, Dublin, Wicklow and Wexford. Special signs were put up and wardens were on duty to ask people to avoid the nesting areas in May and June. Now the terns can nest in peace.

WICKLOW NATIONAL PARK?

All the national parks set up so far are in the west of Ireland – Kerry, Donegal, Connemara and the Burren, Co. Clare. The purpose of these large areas is to protect the landscape and wildlife while providing facilities for visitors to the countryside. The most heavily used mountain area in the country is in Wicklow which is within an hour's drive for most of the million people in Dublin. A recent survey showed that about half the mountain users were from Dublin, but one-third were tourists from other countries. Threats to the mountains include litter, dumping, erosion of paths, turf cutting, new forestry, heather burning and quarrying. A new national park in County Wicklow has been suggested as a way to protect the mountains for future use.

BATTLE FOR THE BADGER

A new programme of killing badgers has been started by the government in an attempt to control the spread of the TB disease among cattle. Hundreds of badgers have been trapped but only a small proportion were found to be carriers of the disease. Many farmers have taken the

The little tern.

law into their own hands and started digging out the badgers' homes or setts and killing the unfortunate badgers. Recent evidence from Britain shows that it is impossible to eradicate TB in the badger population. Instead, more efforts should be made to reduce contacts between cattle and infected badgers. Gassing of setts may be causing the disease to spread to unaffected areas by forcing infected badgers out to join other groups.

SEA EAGLE FLIES FREE

White-tailed sea eagles were widespread on the coasts of Britain and Ireland a hundred years ago. By 1916 all had been shot, trapped or poisoned and the species had become extinct in both countries. Only stuffed eagles and egg collections remained and these can still be seen in the National Museum. Now, after seventy years, the first sea eagle to be hatched in the wild has flown from its secret nest in Scotland. Over eighty young eagles have been collected from wild nests in Norway, where the species is doing quite well, and released on a Scottish Nature Reserve. Most of these are now mature and more pairs are expected to breed in the next few years. Some have even been seen in Ireland recently.

GARDEN PLANT PEST

Rhododendron was introduced to Irish gardens in the last century from its native habitat in the mountains of Asia. Its large pink or purple flowers adorned many old estates but unfortunately it escaped over the garden walls and invaded the woods and bogs nearby. A hundred years later it has become a serious pest in some of the last surviving oakwoods in the country. Its large evergreen leaves cast a dense shade over the ground beneath the oak trees preventing the acorns from developing into young trees. To ensure that the old oaks are replaced as they die a programme of eradicating rhododendron from some of our national parks has begun. This will take many years to complete.

A HIDDEN VOICE
Filming Corncrakes

by Éamon de Buitléar

You know what a ventriloquist is don't you? It is a person who can throw his or her voice and make it sound as if it is coming from somewhere else. Many people believe that the corncrake possesses this wonderful gift and if you try following that elusive bird as I have, you will most probably end up thinking that there really is something magical about him.

Trying to take pictures of a corncrake can drive the most patient photographer quite out of his or her mind! Just imagine yourself on the trail of the invisible actor whose loud rasping 'crek-crek-crek' seems to be coming from three different places, and just when you think you have pinpointed the bird, up comes the sound again in a very different part of the field. This can go on for quite some time until eventually it becomes a game of guess where I am or where I am not!

The first sign of the corncrake's whereabouts is most often the sound of its voice. Although you may not succeed in catching a glimpse of this slender, brown bird with its barred flanks and chestnut wings, if it is in your area you must surely hear it.

The answer to the ventriloquist's trick, which the corncrake seems to play on us, is quite simple. As the bird calls it keeps walking through the meadow, sometimes moving towards you and at other times moving across the field away from you. You cannot see him of course as he is hidden by the grass and so the impression is that the voice is here, there and everywhere, which in a way is true!

Last summer when I was hoping to take some more attractive pictures of a calling corncrake, I set up my hide in a meadow near a ditch, where one particular bird was keeping the countryside awake with a craking voice that sounded like a fly-fisherman's salmon reel. Inside my canvas hide, where I sat hidden from the rest of the world, I had a fine view of the whole field. There were masses of colourful wild flowers everywhere. My camera was pointing out through the peep hole and I waited for the corncrake to move closer. I could hear him away across the meadow calling away to whoever might listen. But why all the noise? The real reason for the unmusical crake was of course to announce his presence, both for the benefit of his mate and as a warning to other male corncrakes to keep out of his territory. 'This is my meadow and nobody else's,' he calls.

Eventually the voice became much louder as the bird moved closer and closer to my hiding place. Although I craned my neck to peer through the various flaps and through my lens, I could see no sign of the

Few people under twenty have ever heard the corncrake.

corncrake. The sound was now so loud that it seemed to be coming from almost inside my hiding place. But yet, I could see no sign of this walking fishing reel. At last I located him. He was standing somewhere at the back of my hide. I could not see him of course but he was so close to me. I could have almost grabbed him by shoving my hand out under the canvas. Alas, there was nothing I could do. The bird had picked a narrow strip of ground between the ditch and my hide and it was the only spot where I could not see him. It was the end of film-making for that day. If I moved now the bird would get such a fright that he might leave the meadow altogether and even if I could turn the camera around there was no hope of filming him in such a narrow space. So with my ventriloquist friend no more than fifteen centimetres away and as invisible as ever, I sat cramped for what seemed hours with no pictures and having to put up with the sweet strains of 'crek-crek-crek, crek-crek-crek, crek-crek-crek'.

WOULD YOU BELIEVE IT?
New research on Nature in Ireland

Compiled by Richard Nairn

SAILING JELLY

Every summer shoals of a strange bluish jellyfish appear on the south and west coasts of Ireland. Known commonly as the by-the-wind-sailor these animals are about eight centimetres across and have a horny skeleton equipped with a soft transparent 'sail'. Just like a yacht, the jellyfish is blown across the ocean by the wind, thus helping it disperse from its birth place. Strangely, most of the 'sailors' found on Irish shores have the 'sail' lying to the right of the body, although occasionally some are found with a left-hand sail. It is likely that the prevailing wind sorts out the two kinds and sends mostly right-hand sailors into Irish waters. (McGrath, *Irish Naturalists' Journal* 1985)

CITY SLEEPERS

On cold winter nights over a thousand pied wagtails roost in the trees down the centre of Dublin's O'Connell Street. Roosting in large numbers is quite common behaviour for many birds such as starlings, thrushes and waders. Individuals are safer from predators this way, because some birds would always be alert while others are sleeping. The pied wagtails, however, are also taking advantage of city centre temperatures, which are about two degrees higher than the surrounding countryside. In the coldest winter weather the birds congregate in the trees near the middle of the street and avoid the more draughty ends of the street. Even the bright Christmas lights do not bother them, but may add to their 'central heating'. (Cotton and Lovatt, *Irish Birds* 1985)

SEASIDE SUPPERS

Otters feed quite commonly on the coast of Ireland as well as on inland rivers and lakes. The evidence is found in the 'spraints' or droppings which the otters leave in prominent positions along the shore as a form of communication. The spraints can be collected and dried and the hard parts of the food items separated out and identified. On the west coast a wide range of salt-water fish is eaten with rocklings, wrasse and eels the most common. Almost any suitable small prey will be taken, including crabs, shellfish, frogs and even birds. The otters prefer to leave their spraints on grassy banks near the mouth of freshwater streams where they go to drink. (Murphy and Fairley, *Irish Naturalists' Journal* 1985)

An otter searches for a tasty meal.

BANDED BRENT

In 1984 an Irish expedition to arctic Canada rounded up some flocks of brent geese on their breeding grounds and put large numbered plastic bands on their legs before releasing them again. Like car registration numbers, each band has a different three-letter code which can be identified up to 250 metres away. In the following two winters almost three-quarters of these marked birds have been recognised around the Irish coast. Individual birds could be followed from one estuary to another. One remarkable traveller was seen in County Down, County Dublin and County Kerry, all within one week in October 1985. While most goose families remain together over the winter, several pairs did separate but later reunited and nested successfully the following summer. (O'Briain, *IWC News* 1986)

RIVER FOREST

When the level of the reservoir on the River Lee in County Cork is lowered, a strange watery wilderness is revealed for all to see. Known as the Gearagh this was once a lovely oakwood interlaced with streams and islands until it was almost all cut down in 1954 for a hydro-electric scheme. The small area which remains has an amazing mixture of woodland and wetland plants. Some of the ancient oak and ash trees reach eighteen metres in height and are covered in mosses and ferns. There is nothing quite like the Gearagh anywhere else in Ireland or Britain, but some similar watery forests still survive along the River Rhine between France and Germany. (White, *Irish Naturalists' Journal* 1985)

WILD BIRDS IN WINTER

The newly published *Atlas of Wintering Birds in Britain and Ireland* gives some interesting information on the birds which visit these islands between November and February. Blackcaps which were once a rarity in winter are now quite common, especially in towns and suburbs, where they feed on bird tables. Redwings, smaller relatives of our song thrush, move into Ireland from continental Europe in enormous numbers in cold weather. Some waders such as lapwing and golden plover are more common on farmland than on the coast in winter. Over 10,000 bird-watchers took part in this survey between 1981 and 1984. The *Atlas* contains a full page map for each of 192 bird species.

The Unicorn was a Narwhal

Story by Fred Bruemmer

Long ago, in the Middle Ages, people believed in unicorns. They thought the unicorn looked like a large deer with one long, twisted, ivory horn growing from its forehead.

The trouble was nobody had ever *seen* a unicorn. People only heard rumours about it from traders and explorers. But they believed the animal must live on earth, because they had seen its horn.

Unicorn horns were very valuable. Each one was worth many times its weight in gold. The reason for this was the belief that a unicorn's horn had miraculous power – it could make poison harmless. So emperors, kings and princes, who worried that someone might poison them, were only too glad to pay large sums of money for drinking cups made from the wonderful horn of the unicorn.

Today we know that no such animal as the unicorn ever existed. But where did those long horns come from? They came from whales!

These whales are called narwhals (NAR-walls), and they live only near the North Pole, in the remotest regions of the arctic seas. They are rare animals. Scientists say there are only about 20,000 narwhals in the world.

Narwhals are small members of the whale family. They grow to be 4 to 5 metres (about 16 feet) long. A narwhal baby, which is called a calf, is 1.5 metres long. A newborn calf is dark slate blue. As it grows older, its colour changes and becomes lighter. Its back remains dark, the sides are spotted black and white and the belly is greyish white.

Only the male grows a horn, which is really a giant, overgrown, left front tooth. It grows straight out through the narwhal's upper lip. It is spiralled and twisted like a corkscrew, and can be 3 metres long. This tooth (or *tusk,* as it is usually called) is hollow. The hollow centre is filled with spongy pulp and nerves, just like your teeth. Occasionally someone sees a narwhal with a broken tusk with the end open and often inflamed. He may be suffering from a giant-size toothache!

What does the male narwhal do with his beautiful tusk? There are many theories. Do they use their tusks like swords to fight each other? Do they use them to poke holes in the polar ice? Probably not, because the tusks may break off if they're used as swords or giant icepicks.

Another theory is that the narwhals use their tusks to spear cuttlefish, squid and crustaceans – which they like to eat. If this is true, then catching food would be difficult for the females, who have no tusks. The most widely accepted theory is that a male uses his tusk in courtship display. But no one really knows for sure.

A few years ago, I lived for six months with the Eskimos of northwestern Greenland, the northernmost people in the world. Narwhals, which are more numerous in this region than anywhere else in the Arctic, are very important to these Eskimos. They hunt them in skin-covered boats called kayaks (KY-aks).

Narwhals, meat and blubber are an important food for the Eskimos and their sled dogs. Eskimos also eat raw narwhal skin, called *muktuk.* You get most of the vitamins you need from fruit and vegetables, but Eskimos live in the far north, where there are no fruit or vegetables. They get vitamins by eating *muktuk.* A chunk of raw narwhal skin contains a lot of vitamin C – as much as a lemon or an orange. Raw *muktuk* is crunchy and tastes like hazelnuts. It is one of the greatest treats for Eskimo children.

The narwhal provides Eskimos with more than food. They dry its tendons to make a tough thread for sewing skin and fur clothing. And from the tusk they carve tools, hunting weapons and toys for their children.

In the summer, herds of narwhals swim underneath ice patches from one open area of water to the next, far into bays and fiords. They stay in the bays until solid sheets of ice begin to form in the autumn. Then, since they are mammals and must surface every ten minutes or so to breathe, they have to leave the bays. They swim to Arctic Ocean areas which, because of strong currents, never freeze over, not even in the coldest winter.

Sometimes, though, a herd of narwhals gets trapped in a bay. A broad band of ice freezes across the bay's entrance. The ice is so wide that the narwhals can't hold their breath long enough to swim underneath it. They would drown before they reached the open sea beyond.

Every day, as it gets colder and colder, more ice covers the bay. Ice moves in on the narwhals from all sides. Finally there is only a small breathing hole of open water left.

For a long time, the splashing of the desperate narwhals prevents the hole from freezing over completely. But then it may become so cold that – no matter how much the narwhals splash and struggle – the hole freezes shut.

If the narwhals can't surface to breathe they will die. But arctic ice shifts and strains, and sometimes a network of wide cracks crisscrosses it. When such a crack reaches the trapped narwhals, they can follow it and swim out again to the freedom of the open sea.

Free of the ice, the narwhals surface to breathe and exhale with a shrill whistle. When they swim fast, they lift their sleek, dark heads high above the surface. Then the tusks of the males flash in the sun as they surge forward – unicorns of the Arctic.

What is the newest mammal discovered in Ireland?

In 1964 a research student was studying small mammals in County Kerry when he trapped a reddish brown rodent with a rounded nose and a much shorter tail than the ordinary field mouse. This was the first-ever record of a bank vole in Ireland. Although voles are common in Britain and other European countries it was thought that none had ever crossed the sea to Ireland. Further investigation showed that bank voles also lived in leafy hedges and woods in Counties Limerick, Clare and Cork and that they were spreading rapidly into new territories at a rate of about up to four kilometres per year. It is now estimated that the bank vole was introduced (possibly from a ship) on the Shannon estuary in County Limerick sometime between 1945 and 1960. It may take another hundred years to spread throughout the rest of Ireland.

Why do birds drop shells from the air?

Have you ever watched a gull or a crow feeding on shellfish on the sea shore? Sometimes they will fly up into the sky with the mussel or cockle shell and drop it from a great height. When it hits the ground the bird will swoop down, pick up the shell and repeat the behaviour a number of times. Eventually the shell will smash on a rock and the bird will eat the soft flesh inside. This method of feeding has evolved because the birds are unable to open the shells which are held tightly closed by a strong muscle inside.

Can turtles live in Irish waters?

Several kinds of turtle have been caught alive around the coast of Ireland. The commonest is the leathery turtle, so-called because its hard shell looks like black leather and is shaped like an up-turned boat. These turtles are huge reptiles up to two metres in length from the horny beak to the tip of the hind flippers. The long front flippers act like paddles and enable them to swim many thousands of miles on annual migration. They are commonest in tropical waters on both sides of the Atlantic Ocean where they lay their eggs in holes dug in sandy beaches. Almost every summer there are reports of leathery turtles caught in fishing nets or the ropes of lobster pots around the Irish coasts. Sometimes the turtles are hauled ashore where they die a slow painful death in the hot sun. They are harmless creatures and should be released in their natural habitat, the sea.

Can plants eat animals?

Most plants get the minerals they need from the soil in which they grow. But the sundew grows in poor boggy ground where minerals are scarce, so it must collect these essential foods in a different way. Each of its leaves is surrounded by a ring of tiny hairs. On the end of each hair is a drop of sticky liquid. When an insect lands on the leaf these hairs curl inwards and trap the insect. The liquid prevents the victim from escaping and helps to digest the flesh which is then absorbed by the plant. Sundew leaves are often slightly red and grow flat on the ground.

WONDER?

It is now estimated that the bank vole was introduced possibly from a ship, on the Shannon Estuary in County Limerick sometime between 1945 and 1960.

When an insect lands on the leaf of this sundew plant, its leaves curl inwards and trap the insect.

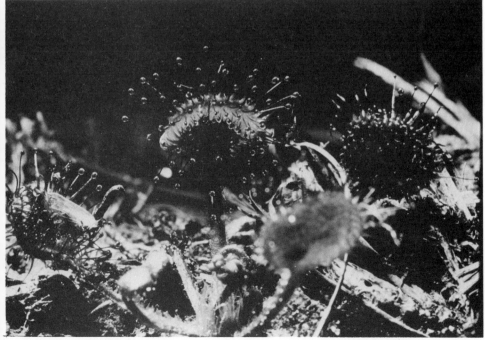

Where have all the corncrakes gone?

An investigation by Richard Nairn

In the year 1900, the corncrake was described by the famous naturalists Richard Ussher and Robert Warren as 'a well known bird fairly numerous in every part of Ireland'. By the 1980s it has vanished from most of the eastern part of the country and also from many of its old strongholds in the west. What has caused this decline and will the corncrake soon be extinct?

Hayfields are the best habitats

Few people aged under twenty have ever heard a corncrake. But older country people have strong memories of the loud 'crake-crake' call which used to keep them awake at night. The corncrake is a secretive bird and spends most of its time hidden in long grass. It usually nests in or near hayfields and during the harvest both nests and young may be destroyed by mowing machines. Some people have suggested that the change to silage-making with earlier mowing has caused the decline in corncrakes. But this is not the complete answer because in some silage-making areas the birds survive and in some places where hay-making continues the corncrake is just a memory.

Marshland drainage

In the early summer before the grass is long enough to hide them, corncrakes are often heard calling in marshy ground where the tall yellow flag iris provides good cover from predators. Farmers have been draining these marshes to improve the land for cattle. Perhaps the loss of the yellow flags has meant a shortage of essential habitat for corncrakes. As the birds die out they may even be too widely scattered to find mates for breeding.

Migration through deserts

Problems for the corncrake do not end in Ireland. Each autumn they undertake a hazardous 6000-mile flight to their winter grounds in southeast Africa. Little is known of them in this area but at least their habitat is not under serious threat. On migration the corncrake must pass through the Sahara desert. The recent increase in size of the desert caused by drought and poor farming methods in places like Ethiopia and Sudan may prevent some corncrakes returning to Ireland to breed.

Crash-landings cause concern

It is known that corncrakes can be killed by colliding with overhead power lines. As they usually fly by night they are attracted to lighthouses and may be killed there too. A century ago hundreds of corncrakes could be seen in May flying around the Arklow lightship in the Irish Sea. Nowadays the sighting of even one corncrake on the east coast would be a rare occurrence.

What can be done to save them?

The Irish Wildbird Conservancy is studying the last remaining corncrakes to find the most suitable habitats for them to breed. Advice is given to landowners to encourage farming methods which benefit the birds. If you have heard a corncrake, write to the IWC at this address – Southview, Church Road, Greystones, Co. Wicklow.

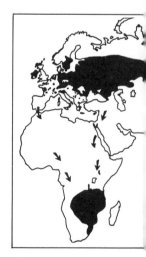

This map shows the two migration routes between corncrakes' northern breeding grounds and their main wintering area in southern Africa.

FOXES

Secretive and nocturnal, foxes eat a wide variety of food including grass, beetles, berries, worms, birds and rodents. Town foxes sometimes rummage through dustbins in search of scraps. Foxes sleep during the day under shrubs, in dry ditches or in disused rabbit or badger holes.

Usually solitary, dog foxes and vixens court and mate amid loud barks and screams in the heart of winter. Cubs, usually four or five, are born in spring and only leave their underground home, the earth, to play when they are a month old.

Sometimes a fox will take over a rabbit's burrow by eating the occupants, or a badger's sett by driving the owners out with a foul smell from scent glands under the tail! In towns they may sleep under a garden shed or seat.

By late summer the vixen no longer looks after the cubs and will ignore them or chase them away. Young vixens will stay in the area of their parents, but young dog foxes are encouraged to move away to new areas by adult foxes. They may have to travel 30 km to find a place where they can set up a territory unchallenged.

Foxes mark out their territories with their scent glands or by leaving droppings or urine in particular places. Also, loud eerie screams are used to ward off other foxes. Look for fox footprints in snow or mud. With four toes and a hind pad, these are rather like those of a small dog. But the pads are narrower and smaller and closer together, giving a narrower print.

At that very moment a huge grey cat sprang to the top of the fence and jumped down into the yard. Immediately the air was filled with shrill warning cries from Mr and Mrs Robin. Number One crouched low in the grass and stayed very still. The other three stayed hidden on the tree branch.

We rushed for the garden hose, hoping to scare off the cat with a spray of water, but Mrs Robin was quicker. She ran along the ground, a few feet ahead of the cat, fluttering her wing. Mr Robin hovered above, beating his wings and scolding the cat with sharp cries.

The cat paused for a second to look up at Mr Robin, then pounced at Mrs Robin. But quick as a flash she flew up out of his reach. Her fluttering wing had been a trick that drew attention away from the babies. We turned on the hose full force, and the cat leaped away over the fence.

It didn't take long for the young robins to learn their flying lessons well enough to go off on their own. Soon the freckles would disappear from their breasts and they would have orange-red ones like their parents'. They would find their own worms and insects that summer and fly south for the winter.

By now the flowers were blooming, and the days were warm. We were just saying how much we missed our robin family when we looked up into the pear tree and saw Mrs Robin's tail sticking up like a flag from the nest. She was nesting again. From above came Mr Robin's cheery song. Soon we would see a second family of robins born, raised and sent out into the world.

64

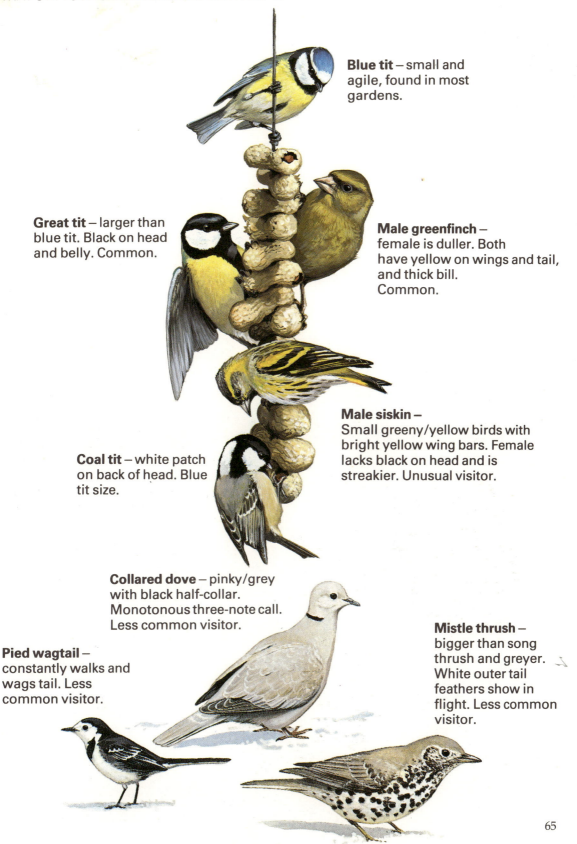

Blue tit – small and agile, found in most gardens.

Great tit – larger than blue tit. Black on head and belly. Common.

Male greenfinch – female is duller. Both have yellow on wings and tail, and thick bill. Common.

Male siskin – Small greeny/yellow birds with bright yellow wing bars. Female lacks black on head and is streakier. Unusual visitor.

Coal tit – white patch on back of head. Blue tit size.

Collared dove – pinky/grey with black half-collar. Monotonous three-note call. Less common visitor.

Mistle thrush – bigger than song thrush and greyer. White outer tail feathers show in flight. Less common visitor.

Pied wagtail – constantly walks and wags tail. Less common visitor.

65

STAMP

Fruit and

OUT

vegetables

by Juanita Browne

The beauty of fruits and vegetables is more than skin deep. When you cut one in half, study the lovely pattern inside. You can use these inner patterns to stamp out prints for decorating many things.

Make your own wrapping paper by stamping designs all over plain paper. Folded greeting cards can have a different fruit on the outside and the inside, paper place mats and kitchen calendars look fine with fruity borders.

And you can stump your friends — have them guess what you used to make your designs. Test yourself on the prints on this page.

You will need poster paints, paintbrushes and paper towels. For prints, newsprint and other absorbent papers work best. (Washable prints on cloth can be made by using acrylic paints or India ink — but don't spill any on your clothes!)

Choose your fruit or vegetable and cut it in half. (Save and eat the part you don't use for printing.) If it is juicy blot gently with paper towels. Carefully paint the cut surface. Press evenly on the paper. Be sure the print is completely dry before using.

Which fruits and vegetables made these prints — the onion, apple, cucumber, artichoke, pear, lemon or mushroom?

FOCUS ON SWALLOWS

by Chris Mead

Long haul

In the autumn Irish swallows go south to France. They travel down the west coast of France and through eastern Spain into Africa. After flying by day in short stages, they then have to face the Sahara, a crossing of over 1,000 km. They reach South Africa after six or eight weeks. In spring they return further to the east, in about the same time.

Marathon

Swallows' migrations alone account for nearly 10,000 km there and 10,000 km back – but, of course, they also feed on the wing. Even if they flew at 25 kph for only four hours each day, swallows easily fly far enough to go round the world each year.

Which sex?

In spring the male is easily told from the female. His outer tail feathers are very long and thin; the female's are shorter and blunter. The male has darker red on the face, too. Young birds are very much paler on the forehead and throat and their tails are short and blunt.

Slow moult

Swallows moult slowly during the winter, when they are in Africa. All the flight feathers have to be replaced – but they take four months to do it, so that they can always fly efficiently.

Long wings

A healthy swallow weighs about 20 g. A greenfinch weighs 30 g and has wings 90 mm long from the bend to the tip. A swallow's wings, however, are 120 mm long. These much longer wings on a lighter bird show that it depends very much on its power of flight. Its wing length and shape make it very good at feeding on the wing.

Where are they?

They are not found in town and city centres, but swallows are very widespread in Ireland. They prefer farms where animals are kept and often nest in stables with ponies.

Autumn flocks

All the young birds added to the adults make a huge population in autumn. They soon leave the nest sites and gather each evening to roost in reed beds. By August and early September these roosts may have up to 100,000 birds! The young birds learn about their home area before they migrate – vital information for next spring when they return.

Bad weather

To get the best nesting sites, our swallows have to come back early. But the weather might be poor and food hard to find. They collect at lakes and reservoirs where there should be insects even if it is cold. These are the best places for early migrants.

Winter in the mud!

Centuries ago many people thought that swallows spent the winter in mud at the bottom on ponds. There were even pictures of them being dug out or caught in nets. Of course, a swallow in a pond would quickly drown.

Continued on P.76

PALACE IN A POND

by Deborah Cavel Greant

You live in a silver palace, built in a cool green pond. Your stairway is attached to a waving water plant, and your sky is a mirror, reflecting all you see.

Your neighbours are minnows, tadpoles, water boatmen and snails. Sometimes a frog splashes past, or a beetle swims overhead.

What are you?

You are a little creature called a water spider, whose 'palace' is no bigger than a thimble and is about the same shape. This spider builds its home underwater among the weeds and grass that grow a few feet down in quiet ponds of Europe and Asia.

'Well,' you say, 'I thought spiders spun webs!' And so they do, and so does this one! Its palace is the only underwater web in the world.

The water spider's body usually measures about 10 millimetres (1/3 inch) and has long legs. It is covered with dark markings and furry grey hair.

Before spinning its web the little spider must first find just the right building site below the water's surface next to a clump of weeds. It spins a thread and attaches it to one of the weeds near the bottom of the pond. The spider then pulls the thread up to the surface and attaches it to the weed at the spot where it leaves the water. This thread is a 'handrail' the spider will use to go up and down quickly.

Back near the bottom, the spider spins more threads, attaching them to nearby weeds to form a rectangle. Inside this framework the spider weaves a tight little carpet. When the carpet is finished the spider goes 'hand over hand' up the handrail to the surface.

Now the spider turns around and sticks its abdomen above the water. Quickly it jerks its abdomen down with a *plop* and traps a silvery bubble of air underneath. Then, holding onto the bubble with its back legs, the spider climbs down the rope.

Once underneath the carpet, the spider turns head up and the bubble slides out, catching under the carpet. The spider brushes off tiny bubbles that cling to its body hair, and adds them to the larger bubble.

Up the handrail and back again with another bubble goes the spider, until the carpet bulges up into a thimble shape. Now the spider has a dry home with an all-around view. When the air supply gets stale, the spider goes up top for a fresh bubble or two.

The water spider catches and eats tiny fish, tadpoles and insects. During the day it sits with its front legs outside the bubble, rushing out if any prey comes close. The spider brings its catch back into its bubble house to eat.

At night it leaves its home to hunt. Though it can hold its breath for 20 minutes at a time, it cannot breathe underwater. This is why the spider always brings its catch back home.

The male water spider is twice as large as the female, which is unusual, for most male spiders are much, much smaller than their mates. The female spider lays 50–100 eggs after mating and wraps them in a silk bag, which takes up the top half of her home. Three to four weeks later the baby spiders chew through the bag and wait for their mother to bring them tiny insects to eat. They grow quickly and before long the house is far too crowded for so many.

The time has come for the little ones to build their own silver palaces. They leave the bubble house. Some stay in the same pond, others climb the 'handrail', crawl out onto a tall weed and spin a thread. The wind catches the thread like a kite, and the little spider goes whizzing away. The lucky ones will drift to a new pond. The unlucky ones will die.

When winter comes and ice covers the pond, the water spider builds a winter bubble in a deep part of the pond. Its summer house had no door, but for the winter house the spider spins a door from the inside, making the house snug and cosy. Then it curls up into a tight ball and goes to sleep until spring.

WHAT NO SEABIRDS? LOOK FOR SEALS!

by Richard Nairn

Seals are among the largest of our wild mammals but they spend at least half of their lives out of sight beneath the waves. On most Irish shores there is a chance of seeing a seal. There are two different species of seals in Ireland.

The **grey seal** is found mostly on the west and south coasts. It is usually seen on wild rocky headlands and islands often beneath cliffs. The white-coated pups are born in September and October and remain on the beaches for up to three weeks. There are about 2,000 grey seals in Ireland and they are often blamed for falling numbers of salmon which is caused by overfishing.

The **common seal** is more usually seen in sheltered waters such as estuaries, bays and harbours. It will lie out of the water on sandbanks or weed-covered rocks when the tide is low. Common seal pups are dark coloured and can swim within hours of their birth. They are born in June and July. There are at least 1,500 common seals in Ireland with the biggest herds in Strangford Lough, Co. Down.

Grey seal

72

Grey seal
hauled out on
rocks

Both species of seals return to their traditional breeding places every year at pupping time. For the rest of the year they may wander hundreds of miles in search of food and could turn up on almost any coast. Sometimes they swim up rivers after fish but they rarely leave salt water.

Fortunately the best features for identifying seals are on the head which is often all you can see when they are in the water. The pattern of the coat varies in each species. Grey seals have large spots – females have pale spots on dark fur and males have dark spots on light fur. Common seals have denser, smaller, dark spots. The grey seal has a big, long, flat head, slightly roman-nosed in males and slightly upcurved in females; the nostrils

are large, set apart and tend to be nearly parallel. The common seal has a smaller head, with a more rounded top and short snout so the head is shaped more like a cat's; the nostrils are closer together and the lower ends come together in a V.

When they dive grey seals roll over showing their backs as they go under; common seals show less. Both dive brilliantly and swim very well and very fast underwater; they can stay under for 15 minutes or more.

There are many stories and legends about seals. Their large eyes and lonely cries have led to the belief that they are drowned seamen returned in a different form. In reality, seals are intelligent and sensitive wild creatures and they deserve to be left in peace.

Common seals

Answers to Wildlife Quiz on page 46

1. A gosling.
2. A young eel.
3. A form.
4. Chlorophyll.
5. Nettle.
6. The Beaufort scale.
7. The three species of wild deer found in Ireland.
8. A female fox.
9. They don't build nests. They lay in the nests of other birds.
10. A cygnet.
11. A sett.
12. Because it feeds on rats and mice.
13. No. It is a hard, woody, marble-sized lump which grows on oak trees when a tiny gall wasp lays its eggs in a bud.
14. Types of ferns.
15. The mayfly.
16. Yes.
17. In oysters.
18. Linen.
19. A stone used by a thrush to smash snail shells against.
20. The bat.
21. No. It reflects sunlight.
22. To scan the ground for food.
23. Types of geese.
24. The hermit crab.
25. The egg-case of a dogfish or skate.
26. The gannet.
27. The pygmy shrew.
28. The swift.
29. The red deer on land or the blue whale in the sea.
30. The goldcrest.
31. False: they live on the floors of houses.
32. A type of amphibian.
33. Seven.
34. Eight; some have six.
35. A seabird like a small graceful gull.
36. The frog-hopper nymph, a small jumping bug.
37. The sedge warbler.
38. The salmon.
39. A common spring flower of damp meadows.
40. A tropical drift seed that is carried to Irish coasts by ocean currents.

THE
INCH WORM — Siv Cedering Fox

inches across
the green, green leaf,
Should I squash him?

eating a hole in the cabbage
head,
Should I crush him?

moving his many legs
across a branch,

Should I push him?

slowly wiggling down
the walk,

Should I step on him?

He could become a butterfly
and I could catch him.

He could have orange and black
and golden wings,

and I could watch him.
He could feed a hungry robin
if I leave him

inching,

inching.

The same ones?

Many people think that the same pair of swallows has nested in their shed or porch for years. But each adult swallow has only a 50:50 chance of surviving to come back next year. Sometimes one will make it, and find a new mate. If both die, the site will be taken over by other swallows if it is a good one.

Cheat!

There is a story about a man in ancient Rome who caught the swallows at his home and took them to the chariot races. When the race had finished he tied coloured threads, showing who had won, to the swallows' legs and let them go. They flew straight back to the nest where the servants could see them – and place bets on the race before anyone thought it was possible to know who had won!

The green cross code

Many swallows are killed by cars. But ringing recoveries show that swallows do learn about cars as they get older. Of all the young birds reported dead, over a third have been run over. But only an eighth of the swallow equivalent of teenagers (first year birds) and a twelfth of adults are killed on the roads.

For their size cuckoos lay small eggs, but they match fairly closely the size of the eggs they mimic. It is not known whether a cuckoo will pick the same host species as its parent did but, as they tend to return to the same area each year, this seems quite likely.

By laying its egg while the host is still laying its own, the cuckoo makes sure that all of the eggs are incubated at the same time. Cuckoos' eggs take an unusually short time to hatch – only about 11 days – so that the young parasite usually hatches a day or two before the host's own eggs. The blind, naked and helpless cuckoo then does an amazing thing. Although a host's egg weighs as much as itself, it nudges it to the side of the nest and then uses its legs, back and wings to push it up the side of the nest and over the edge. It continues with each egg until the nest is empty.

Cuckoos eat mainly insects, taking a wide variety of larvae as well as centipedes, spiders, ants, worms and slugs which they find on or near the ground. Their favourite food is caterpillars and they will gorge themselves on brightly coloured, hairy caterpillars which are avoided by other birds because they are poisonous. These are swallowed whole and broken down by the cuckoo's digestive system. Because young cuckoos must be fed on insects, all the birds chosen as hosts are insect eaters. Although the insect food given to the young cuckoo will often be quite unlike the food of the adult, when it becomes independent it instinctively feeds on caterpillars.

Because they do not care for their own young, adult cuckoos can migrate south early, and begin to leave in July. The young leave about a month later but often remain here until September. Before migration was properly understood, people believed that cuckoos hibernated in tree-stumps, or even that they returned into hawks in winter.

This last idea is not as odd as it seems. Cuckoos, with their long tails and barred underparts, look very like sparrowhawks. Small birds will mob adult cuckoos in the same way as they mob birds of prey, and host species will attack stuffed cuckoos or even tape recorders emitting the male's call.

For most humans though, the cuckoo is an exciting bird and its call seems to confirm that spring has really arrived. Scientists are still studying the cuckoo to unravel all the secrets of its unusual way of life.

You can find a lot more information about cuckoos in Ian Wyllie's book The Cuckoo *published by Batsford.*

Most cuckoos arrive in Ireland in late April and the adults have gone again by the end of July. Young cuckoos may stay until September when they instinctively begin the long journey to Africa.

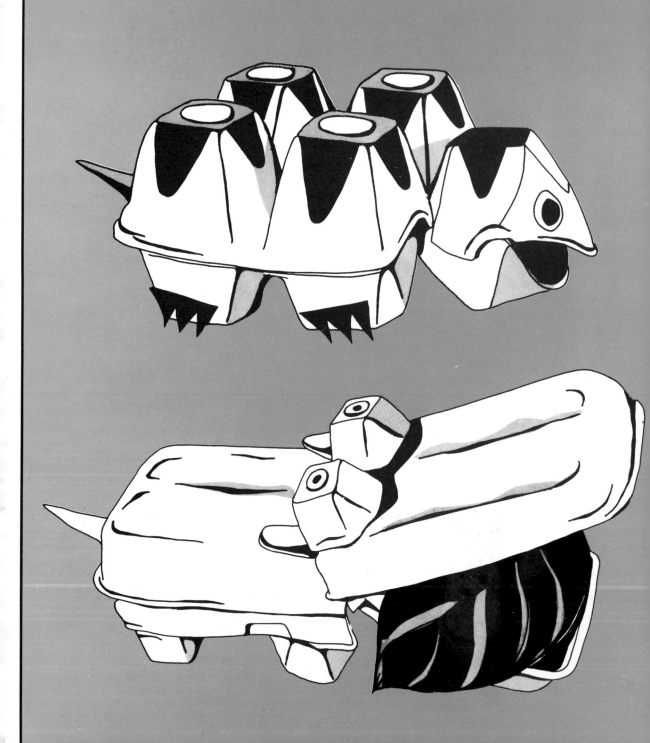

EGG CARTON

by Donna Sterman

Each of these animals (except for the hippo) can be made from one egg carton. The hippo needs two. After you've followed the directions for making these, try creating some of your own egg carton animals.

You'll need:
cardboard egg cartons
(10cm x 15cm with
solid lid)
scissors
white glue
coloured paper
poster paints
stapler (optional)

CREATURES

Hedgehogs eat almost anything they reach, including dead birds. Slugs, caterpillars and beetles are easy to eat, but they have problems with a snail. Most of their prey is found by sound and smell, as the hedgehog's eyesight is not very good. They eat a lot of garden pests. Many of these, as well as many small, harmless animals which make up their natural food, are killed by garden chemicals.

Hedgehogs have a very peculiar habit called self-anointing. They use their tongues to spread frothy saliva over their spines and fur. They twist and turn their bodies into almost impossible positions to do it. No one knows why it is done.

Hedgehogs may not seem to be very agile, but they can climb very well. They can even climb brick walls. If they fall, their spines cushion the shock of landing and they are not harmed. Hedgehogs can swim, though not very well. Many drown in garden ponds and swimming pools, not because they can't swim, but because they are unable to climb out before they are exhausted. A small piece of wire mesh hung over the side will give them a foothold so that they can climb out.

The hedgehog is able to live in the artificial surroundings of towns and housing estates. Nests of newspaper are as good as those made of leaves. They are often made under sheds, in garages or even in an electricity substation like this one. Although this little animal was already around at the same time as the woolly mammoth and the sabre-toothed tiger, it is, unlike them, still doing well now.

Pat Morris's book – *Hedgehogs* (Whittet Books) published in 1983, gives much more information about these animals.